Men in Skirts

Men in Skirts

An Army Medic's Account of the Korean War and After

Richard H. Waltner

Authors Choice Press

San Jose New York Lincoln Shanghai

Men in Skirts
An Army Medic's Account of the Korean War and After

All Rights Reserved © 2000 by Richard H. Waltner

Authors Choice Press
an imprint of iUniverse.com, Inc.

For information address:
iUniverse.com, Inc.
5220 S 16th, Ste. 200
Lincoln, NE 68512
www.iuniverse.com

ISBN: 0-595-15125-6

Printed in the United States of America

This book is dedicated to all the medics and doctors who served in the Clearing Company, 120th Medical Battalion, 45th Infantry Division from March of 1953 to March of 1954.

CONTENTS

ACKNOWLEDGEMENTS

I would like to give thanks to Mr. Robert Grossheider for the many hours spent reading my manuscript, for making corrections and for taking time with me to make suggestions for changes which have increased the readability of this book; to Ms. Sandy Boutin for her expertise and time spent with the computer getting all of the material in the necessary order to be submitted for publication. I would also like to thank my wife Bonnie for faithfully keeping all 460 plus letters I sent her from Korea. Without those letters writing this book would not have been possible. In addition I would like to thank her for reading draft after draft of the manuscript, finding errors and making suggestions for improvement.

INTRODUCTION

Men in Skirts, in its entirety, is written from some 460 plus letters sent to my fiancé, later my wife. We had agreed to write each other daily, and we faithfully did just that. A good number of those letters, short as they may be, were written by the light of my ever trusty Zippo lighter. I have devoted part of one chapter to our meeting, falling in love, becoming engaged, and sustaining that love through nearly 16 months of separation. My wife is really the heroine of this book for having saved those many, many letters.

I cannot adequately describe the experience of re-reading those letters once again 45 years later. I have been gifted with a good memory but, whereas I could recall incidents in broad strokes, I could no longer remember many of the details. Those letters transported me back over 45 years. I relived every experience recounted in the book. Not only that, but also as I read the details of the experiences, I again felt the emotions that coursed through my body at the time of the incident. Again I found myself wanting to hold the hand of the prostitute who was so badly burned. I wanted to stroke her brow, to tell her it would turn out okay, to reassure her when I knew it wouldn't turn out all right. I wanted to cry along with her as she experienced unbelievable pain. Many times I wanted to cry but I couldn't, even when crying would have been so appropriate. I desperately wanted to cry standing in the ambulance surrounded by the bodies of four young men killed just a few days before Christmas of 1953, nearly five months after the cease fire had been in effect. Someone needed to weep. If not for the dead then for the living: the mothers, fathers, wives, sweethearts and children of those men…For in a few days, just before Christmas, they would receive a tragic and totally unexpected Christmas

1

present: a message from the government informing them of the death of their loved one. I could not do the weeping because I could not get beyond the lump in my throat.

I experienced again the anger at being raised in a culture that would not and could not tolerate men who cried. This is a terrible injustice that American culture and society has imposed on its men. Since then I have learned to cry with difficulty but cry nonetheless. My wife and I lost a little daughter shortly after birth. Thirty-five years later, I still think about Robin, about that beautiful baby, and how I was robbed of the joy of fathering her and what she might have become and then the tears and sobs return. I'm glad they do; however, I'm not completely there yet since I make it a point to do my crying in private. I don't want my wife to see me in my moment of "weakness." There were so many reasons for men to cry: physical pain, the loss of a buddy, home sickness, fear. The list goes on and yet, men couldn't cry.

Since the incidents described in this book are lifted directly from the pages of those letters, there is no embellishment here. I tell the incident, and relate the experience as it happened. There is no need to embellish since war is indeed hell. Yes, for the doubters, this description even applies to the Korean War, which has been called various names other than war, police action and Korean conflict to name two. Orwellian newspeak? To be sure. And for the likes of me, I do not know what those who use these substitutes are trying to accomplish. Even more difficult to understand is why so often Korea is left out of the picture. David Gergen, in an editorial in the January 3-10, 2000 issue of U.S. News and World Report, writes, "Prosperous times after World War II lifted American spirits, but they were quickly dampened by the Cold War, Vietnam and Watergate." As is so often the case, there is no mention of Korea. I would venture to say that Korea was disillusionment concomitant to the Cold War and a war equally as horrific as Vietnam. How dare anyone omit it by deeming it to be unimportant? On the other hand, other than those involved in one way or another, perhaps few in the United States really cared that much. I want to remind the reader that this "forgotten war" claimed the lives of approx- imately 54,000 American men and wounded at least another 100,000. How dare anyone refer to it as anything other than what it was, war, war with all its accompanying pain and death and loss, bewilderment and con- fusion and any other emotions that are appropriate.

I trust that the older reader will become aware again and the younger reader, perhaps for the first time, that there was an awful war involving American boys sandwiched between World War II and the Vietnam war, and it took place in what was then an unknown country to most Americans and that country was Korea.

The title, Men in Skirts, may seem rather odd. It is a title that I picked when I first thought about writing a book on my Korean experiences some 47 years ago, many years before the rebirth of the womens' movement of the late 60s and early 70s. It should be remembered that in the period leading up to the 70s, except for the years of World War II, women were believed to be less intelligent than men, incapable of abstract thought, unable to handle responsibility and independence, not allowed to take responsibility for their private lives and more able to follow than to lead. This is precisely the view the Army held of the enlistee and the draftee. It was and still is my unwavering perspective that we were viewed as not being very intelligent, unable to handle responsibility of any kind and, of course, unable to take responsibility for our private lives. In fact, there was no such thing as a private life. To be sure, we were much better suited to follow than to lead. In short, we were men in skirts. Of course, as with the view of women, this view was totally erroneous. One had to constantly fight this image, this mind set if one were not to succumb to it.

I hadn't been in the Army 48 hours when the reality of that mind set hit home. In 48 more hours, I came to the conclusion that it wasn't the enlistee or the draftee who fit the image, who were the stupid ones, very often it was the non-commissioned officers and yes, even many of the officers. On one exceptionally rainy, cold and miserable day, on impulse the Commanding General of the 45th Infantry Division hopped into his helicopter and flew over the medical compound with his binoculars trained on the ground, looking for cigarette butts. When he had spotted a few, he called the Company Commander and ordered an immediate policing up of the area. It made no difference that medics had to leave their posts, which included wards filled with the sick and wounded, that the ground was saturated with water, literally a sea of mud, and that slogging through the mud would leave a mess far worse than a few cigarette butts. The General had commanded and there we were, putting everything else on hold while the area was cleaned of cigarette butts. And then there was the general who flew to Yongdung P'o to welcome replacements to the 45th Infantry Division and ended up having a sergeant led away by two M.Ps. for having the audacity to light up a cigar while he was giving his welcoming talk.

If I appear to be critical of and hard on the Army, I fully intend to be so. So much of the stupidity was totally unnecessary. I was fortunate to be in the medics where very often the officers were doctors. Drafted doctors were doctors first and officers second. They had to play soldier to be soldiers. Doctors who were career officers were more likely than not cut from a different piece of cloth. They were Army first and doctors second. I can only imagine what it was like in non-medical units. Of course 47 years later the Army may have undergone profound change. I am writing about the Army I knew almost 50 years ago.

Am I alone in my thinking, in my criticism? I think not. The very last thing I had to do before leaving the Army was listen to a captain drone on and on about the advantages and benefits of re-enlisting. There were thousands of men in a very large auditorium, all about ready to go home. As the captain was delivering his speech, the room got so noisy that he had to order silence. I clearly recall him saying, "I don't want to give this talk, but I have to and since I have to you are going to listen." Later I heard that only a very few out of thousands re-enlisted.

Nothing in this book is meant to offend. At the same time I must warn that some may be offended. I have included a chapter on sex and the military. Few books written on men at war include this topic, yet to ignore sex in the military is to be patently dishonest. It was, and I imagine still is, a big problem both for the military and for the men and women who make up the institution. No where is the conservatism of the Army more apparent than in its efforts to deal with the sexuality of the soldier, individually and collectively. And, to say the least, some of the measures taken by the Army I knew were both ridiculous and without merit.

In the Beginning

On June 25th, 1950, I was working for two elderly bachelor brothers in the wheat fields of Kansas. As was their custom, there was no work on the Sabbath. The Sabbath was for worship and resting. As a rule, I accompanied the two brothers to church services. For some reason, on this particular Sunday morning, the two young women who kept house and cooked for Adolph and Joe and the hired hands and, who seldom missed church services did not accompany us to church. It was a rule that after church we would go home to a feast fit for a king. As we made the short drive home, I anticipated the noon meal. Back in those days, girls learned early from their mothers how to cook. Marjean and Darda had learned their culinary skills well.

As we drove in the driveway, both girls came running from the house to greet us. They were yelling something. I couldn't make out what they were saying until Adolph turned the ignition off on his Dodge. "We are at war!" they cried. "North Korea invaded South Korea today and now we are at war." At that moment, although the trip itself would be two years in the future, I knew I would be going to Korea. The feeling was overwhelming and unexplainable. It was as if a voice spoke to me saying, "You will be going to Korea." Not once did I question that early revelation. I knew that in time I would be drafted and that I would be going to Korea. Whereas many of the men I took basic training with hoped and prayed for European or stateside duty at the completion of basic, I never gave much thought to the possibility that I would be going anywhere but to Korea. So after basic training, when orders were cut and received and mine read FECOM (Far East Command), I was not in the least bit disappointed nor worried. What caused me some concern was the forthcoming 18 day trip by boat, first to Japan and then to Korea. I had a problem with motion sickness, and I feared that those 18 days would be rough ones and, indeed they were.

Before any of this would transpire, however, I had another year of college to finish and a summer to be spent in the U.S. Forest Service in the panhandle of Idaho. It was a lot like playing a waiting game. I knew that one day I would find in my mailbox a letter that started with, "Greetings from the President of the United States..." Just when, I wasn't sure, but by keeping track of who, from my home community, was being drafted month by month, I knew when my turn was getting close.

After I had completed my second year of college and spent the summer of 1951 in Idaho, all plans came to an end. It was necessary to find a job since life went on, but that too was a short-term arrangement. Then in July of 1952, the letter finally arrived. I was to report for induction into the U.S. Army in Sioux Falls on September 17th. The final count down began. I can't say I didn't experience times of discouragement. I really wasn't enamored of being drafted into the Army and since I had heard so many negative comments about basic training, I certainly wasn't looking forward to it. Yet, I carried no illusions with me; I was going to Korea. However, before the 17th of September, an event happened in my life to change it forever. I met and fell in love with the girl of my dreams.

Bonnie, The Love of My Life, My Sweetheart, My Wife (and Rick)

This, of course, is not a love story; however, a deep and abiding love was omnipresent during the 16 months in Korea. There is no way I could pen these lines without talking about Bonnie. She played too vital a role in my life. It was Bonnie who gave me promise that there was life beyond Korea. It was Bonnie who lifted my spirits when they sagged. It was Bonnie who helped me through the down times and believe me, there were down times. It was Bonnie who forced my attention away from Korea and off myself. In letter after letter she shared the wedding plans she was so faithfully making with full confidence there would be a wedding. It was my commitment to and love for her that kept me from straying from the straight and narrow path while in Japan, and believe me there were times when the temptations were almost overwhelming. And, it was Bonnie who faithfully kept every letter I wrote her. Without those approximately 460 letters, writing this book would have been impossible. I was never too tired to write her a daily letter telling her of the day's events. I thought I remembered most of what I experienced in Korea; however; re-reading those letters written some 47 years ago revealed to me just how much I had forgotten, especially the details. This manuscript is a distillation of what I consider to be important events in my life while in Korea and recorded in detail in those 460 letters. I pull no punches and I make no omissions because some might feel uncomfortable. I tell it the way it was and as it was recorded in those letters.

I met Bonnie just three weeks before my induction into the Army at Fort Sheridan, Illinois. Our meeting was more than mere chance. I believe this firmly. I lived in south east South Dakota, and Bonnie lived in north east Nebraska. We both belonged to the same Protestant denomination. Three weeks before leaving home for the Army, on a Sunday morning, I traveled to Nebraska to be present at the services in the rural church to which Bonnie belonged. I arrived early so I waited in my car as members began arriving. A car pulled up and a tall young woman stepped out. She was wearing a basic white, one-piece dress with small gray patterns. She was also wearing a white hat. In the early 50s, women wore hats for most occasions. Flowing out of that hat was the most beautiful black hair (my preference in women has always been dark hair) framing a most attractive and unblemished face. I had not wanted to travel to Nebraska that Sunday morning. With departure for the Army just three weeks away, I had lost interest in most local happenings. I guess I would have been content to just sit around and mope. Suddenly that all changed. I just had to meet that young woman. I sat a few pews behind her in church and I couldn't keep my eyes off that dark, dark hair. But I was a stranger. How was I going to effect a meeting, a get together? That was solved when after the service I was informed that I would be having dinner with her family. That was too good to be true. When I arrived at her home, I had a good chance to see her up close, and she was even more attractive than the fleeting glimpses I had gotten of her in church revealed.

We were introduced. Her name was Bonnie, and she just happened to be home after completing nurses' training in Omaha. She later told me she was irritated that she would have to entertain when she only had a few days at home before returning to Omaha and her first nursing job. On that Sunday in early August 1952, I fell in love with Bonnie. I mean really in love. No passing infatuation there. She seemed interested in me, and we spent much time talking. Bonnie talked about her years in Omaha and I about my college years, summer in Idaho, etc. We were so relaxed around each other; however, I had no idea what, if anything, she felt for me. I was sure that such an attractive young woman, at the very least, had a steady boy friend. She didn't.

When it was time to return to South Dakota, I did not want to go. Her beauty haunted me for the next couple of days, and I was depressed. At the moment it seemed my date with Uncle Sam precluded any chance to pursue her. I knew she would be home for a week before returning to Omaha. So I called her one evening and asked her for a date. I was so sure she would say she couldn't because of a boyfriend that I almost didn't make that call. I about fell off my perch when she said yes. I was on cloud nine. I determined then and there that since time was short, I would have to work fast. There was no time to waste.

Again I drove to Nebraska, only this time with much anticipation and very positive feelings about developing a relationship with Bonnie. We drove to Norfolk and ate supper in a hotel restaurant. We both ordered what was supposed to have been fresh mountain trout. It had to be the worst trout either of us had ever eaten. And, of course, both of us have eaten many, many trout since that time. We then went to a movie, The Greatest Show on Earth. Although the movie had an all-star cast, I can only remember Charlton Heston and Betty Hutton. After the movie and lunch, we started for Bonnie's farm home. She asked me if I minded taking a shortcut, a back road to her home. Of course, I didn't, and I rightly surmised that she was in no hurry to get home. A few miles from her home we parked. It was then I realized that Bonnie had strong feelings for me, strong enough that we decided to keep in touch once I left for the Army. The sun had risen before I deposited her at the front door of her home. She was the most wonderful girl to kiss, warm, yielding and reciprocating. Now my world had become an exciting and interesting place even though I would soon be in the Army.

And we kept in touch and during the 16 weeks of basic training our relationship deepened and our love for each other grew stronger. In fact, I decided that during the 10 days leave time from Camp Pickett, Virginia, to Camp Stoneman, California, I would give her a diamond. Bonnie told me she anticipated receiving one at that time. On my six-day furlough, 10 with travel time, Bonnie and I spent as much time together as possible. She was working full time at a hospital in Omaha but was able to get a few days off for my homecoming. It was during our time together that I gave her a diamond, which she graciously accepted; we were engaged. We knew we would be separated for at least a year and perhaps more. At it turned out, our separation lasted 16 months. We were, however, committed to each other and we would have to continue our courtship via letters. We had no other choice. Both of us were confident we would be able to do so, and we pledged ourselves to the task facing us.

My train for Camp Stoneman, CA, stopped in Omaha, and that is where I was to embark as well. That enabled Bonnie and I to spend part of my last day of furlough together. We did so talking about our forth-coming separation and looking beyond that to our forth-coming marriage. At the moment, the time of our reunion seemed interminably long.

At 11:00 p.m., we said our goodbyes in Bonnie's apartment, a most painful departure to say the least. I called a cab, it arrived, and in a short time I was on my way to California. It was a bittersweet separation. The length of the separation weighed heavily, but our engagement and plans to marry upon my return presented me with a necessary lift that I badly needed at this time.

Throughout the 16 months I was in Korea, we planned the wedding. I should say that Bonnie did most of the planning. I regretted I could not be home giving her a helping hand. My part consisted mostly of agreeing with Bonnie's plans or suggesting certain changes in those plans. Nonetheless, over the months, the forthcoming wedding was slowly taking shape.

Each of us wrote the other daily. Writing was a poor substitute for being together, but it was the best we could do. Our love for each other did not wane though we discussed the fact that when we finally would meet after the many months of separation we would literally be strangers to each other.

I have looked back at that lengthy separation many times. Absence is said to make the heart grow stronger. In some few cases, maybe yes, but in most cases just the opposite happens. There were a number of situations that came to my attention where that certainly was the case. I wish I could remember the names of all of the friends whose marriages ended primarily because of the long period of separation. But for Bonnie and me absence did make the heart grow stronger. Why did it work for us while it failed for others? We were in love, we had made a commitment to each other and to our relationship, and we were a bit older and maybe a bit more mature than some of my friends. And, we had a pretty clear picture of the future we wanted together. Of course, there were dark moments but never was there any doubt about our going ahead with plans for the wedding once I returned. I don't know in what shape I would have survived those 16 long months if it hadn't been for Bonnie and her daily letters, offering me hope, encouragement and assurance that better days lay ahead for both of us. The separation was tough for her too and when I got to feeling too sorry for myself, I had to remind myself of that fact.

And then one day my tour of duty in Korea was over. After an uneventful, slow boat ride back to the States, I stepped off the ship in Seattle on June 30th, 1954. Since the 4th of July was just around the corner, the personnel at Fort Lewis and Camp Carson had decided to process us 24 hours a day in order to get us on our way home no later than July 2nd. Processing was a continuous ordeal. I recall going 70 hours without sleep. Interestingly, after so many hours without sleep, I felt like I was on a cheap drunk.

Finally at 7:00 p.m., on the evening of July 2nd, I boarded a train in Denver for a slow 11 hour ride to Schuyler, Nebraska. Why Schuyler?

Because it was the closest the train came to Bonnie's home. At 6:00 a.m., the morning of July 3rd, the train stopped in Schuyler, and I was the only one to disembark. I looked around and no one was in sight. In a moment, however, Bonnie came around a corner of the depot and after 16 long months, we were finally once again re-united. And just as we had anticipated, we really were pretty much strangers to each other. The "strangeness," however, didn't last long. Once we were in each other's arms, it fell away like a tattered garment.

On July 11th, two years after we first met, 16 months after our engagement 12 days after I arrived back in the U.S. and nine days after we were re-united in Schuyler, Nebraska, we were married. That was 46 years ago and we are still very much together and very much in love. As a family sociologist, I know that it should never have worked out but it did. It not only worked out but it did so in wonderful and marvelous ways.

A Skirt that Doesn't Fit:
Kicking Against the Pricks

On the 17th of September, with somewhat of a somber resignation to what lay ahead, I boarded a bus at Olivet, South Dakota. My directive read Olivet, the county seat, even though the bus would be coming through Freeman, my home town. That really didn't make sense but there was much about the Army that didn't make sense. A good friend Max Hein also boarded the bus so for at least a few days each of us would keep company with someone who was a friend. My parents took me to Olivet where we said our good byes. Once on the bus, I was not to leave it even though its stop in Freeman was for 10 minutes.

In Sioux Falls, it was easy. There was a large contingent of South Dakota boys. We were all herded into a large room where we took some kind of an oath and with the oath, I was finally, officially in the Army. After the oath taking all of us were given an evening pass and told to be back at 11:00 p.m. The next day I would be boarding a train for the ride to Fort Sheridan, Illinois.

It was at Fort Sheridan that I realized that we recruits were men in skirts, indeed. And this realization hit me very, very soon after arrival. Once I was issued my allocation of G.I. clothing, the civvies in which I arrived at camp had to be sent home. Now it goes without saying that in the military the recruit had no privacy. I had brought with me a small satchel with toiletries, etc., to get me through the first few days in the Army. In that satchel was a barbering kit which, along with a clipper and an assortment of combs, included a straight edge razor. While in college, I had given haircuts to supplement my meager income, and I felt that those

14

tools might come in handy once basic training began. I had no idea that my personal belongings would be gone through without my knowledge until I heard my name over the P.A. (public address) system ordering me to report to the C.P. (Control Post) immediately. What possible reason would anyone have to want to see me in the C.P.? Perhaps some family member had fallen ill in the brief time that I was absent from home.

I entered the C.P., walked up to the desk behind which sat the First Sergeant, and gave what I am sure was a sloppy salute while saying, "Private Waltner reporting as ordered, sir." And then all hell broke loose. "What was I doing with a concealed weapon in my satchel? What did I intend to with that concealed weapon? Didn't I know that in the short time I was in the Army, I had committed a court marshal offense?" No, I didn't know I had committed a court marshal offense, and I asked as politely as I could, "What in the hell are you talking about?" Ah ha! A snooping cadre had found my barbering kit and, of course, the straight edge razor. The concealed and dangerous weapon the sergeant made reference to was my razor. Again and again I tried to explain why I had the razor. I pointed out that it was rolled up in the kit bag along with an assortment of combs, a hair clipper, etc., so it should be obvious why I had the razor and what my intentions for it were. All to no avail. We went through that again and again. "What were my real intentions? Didn't I know I could end up in the stockade right here in Fort Sheridan?" The First Sergeant and the other cadre in the room were jerking me around and having a ball doing it. They knew darn well the razor was part of my barbering kit. They wanted to shake me up and shake me up good. And, in all honesty, I was all shook up. Finally, the First Sergeant said, "All right, we won't have the M.Ps. (military police) come to get you, but I want you to bring all of your civvies here to the C.P. and I will watch you as you wrap each item to be sent home. The straight edge razor will go into one of your shoes, and when every thing is wrapped to my satisfaction, one of the cadre will accompany you to the post office and watch as you mail that razor back to South Dakota." And that is exactly what I did and what they did. That was incident number one. I was treated as if I were a stupid idiot; I was untrustworthy from the word go. First I couldn't be trusted with the razor, and second, I couldn't be trusted to send the razor home without supervision.

The second incident occurred the very next night. It was a Friday and for two days we had been hearing about a G.I. (government issue) party. Now no one told us what a G.I. party was. In our naiveté, we assumed that it was a party thrown for us as new recruits. Wouldn't that be the day? We were told to meet in the barracks after the evening meal and then we would learn what a G.I. party was. We did meet in the barracks and we quickly learned that a G.I. party is an insane effort to scrub through the barracks floor with extremely stiff bristled brushes and lye soap. There would be no going to bed until the floor was scrubbed white which, of course, was an impossibility. Nonetheless, we scrubbed and we scrubbed and no matter how hard we scrubbed, the raw, unfinished floor didn't get any whiter. Finally, sometime after midnight and exhausted, we were told that although we had done a lousy job, we could go to bed.

It was about 3:00 a.m. when a corporal with a giant sized Charlie horse between his ears, recently returned from Korea and staying in one of the cadre rooms in the barracks, came into the barracks stone drunk. He was singing or trying to sing at the top of his voice and, of course, woke everyone. After a few minutes of this, a fellow from west of the River, the Missouri River in South Dakota that is, hollered out at the top of his voice, "Shut up and let us get some sleep." That was the wrong thing for him to say and I knew we were in deep trouble. The corporal came unglued. He demanded to know who told him to shut up. Of course, no one said a word. Again, he wanted to know whom it was that told him to shut up. Silence. "Okay you sons a bitches, all of you roll out of bed, get dressed and fall out in front of the barracks. We are going to double time around the company area until I find out who told me to shut up." And so absolutely bushed, we crawled out of our bunks, got dressed and were about to leave the barracks when a sergeant, who had also recently returned from Korea and was also staying in one of the cadre rooms, came out of his room and demanded to know from the corporal what was going on? The corporal told him, and the sergeant told the corporal that he was crazy and then told us to go back to bed. Being out ranked, the corporal could only grumble, fall into his sack and pass out. That was the second incident that convinced me that we were indeed, men in skirts.

Now I have no intention of talking about basic training, since I am sure that for most G.Is, it was largely the same. However, in order to fix in the minds of the reader why I have chosen such an unusual title for the name of this book, I must relate one further incident.

At Fort Sheridan, I was given orders to report to Camp Pickett, Virginia. Camp Pickett had just re-opened after closing down following World War II and it was in deplorable condition. At the time it was the only Army base at which medics took their 16 weeks of basic training. We had to put up with the usual harassment and crap, which is familiar to all ex G.Is. of the Korean War era, nothing new about that. One day, however, I was on K.P (kitchen police). Right after the noon meal was served, the plumbing in the kitchen plugged up and plugged up good. The Mess Sergeant singled me out and said; "Waltner, go down to the C.P. and tell whoever is on duty to send up a plumber and to do so immediately. We have the evening meal to prepare." And, he added; "You get right back here." I ran to the C.P. and went inside. Inside was the First Sergeant, an intellectual giant to say the least, and our Company Commander at the time, a Lieutenant, who had recently arrived at the Company. Neither acknowledged me, they kept up their conversation. For at least five minutes, I stood at attention waiting for one of the men to address me. It didn't happen. All the while I could hear the Mess Sergeant saying; "You get right back here." Finally I said; "Excuse me sir," addressing Lieutenant, "the Mess Sergeant sent me down here to report plugged plumbing and to ask that you call a plumber." Again, all hell broke loose. The Lieutenant came unglued. I must add that he had a massive black eye. Apparently he had gotten the worst of a fight the night before, was nursing a grudge, and it wasn't hard to tell from the conversation between him and the First Sergeant that he was in a sour mood. "You son of a bitch," he yelled at me. "Who in the hell gave you permission to talk?" Permission to talk? Yep, I had to have permission to talk. Like a dutiful wife or daughter, it was mandatory that I defer to the superior male. About this time the First Sergeant chimed in. Now here was a man who had a difficult time putting a sentence together. He said to the Lieutenant, "Give him hell. Let him know that he can't come in here and speak until and unless he is given permission to do so." And so, both of them kept at me. I don't remember how long they kept it up, but I completely forgot about the Mess Sergeant and his admonition, "You get right back here." Finally they quit. In a state of shock, I dragged myself back to the mess hall. I must have been pale or looked scared or both because the Mess Sergeant asked me what happened. I told him why I was so late in returning, sparing none of the gory details. I guess he figured I had had enough for one day and said nothing but just shook his head. Does anyone still have trouble understanding why I decided so long ago to name this book, MEN IN SKIRTS?

I made up my mind then and there that the Army wasn't going to break me. I could be called every name under the sun, I could be the target of intimidation, but I would not be robbed of my dignity and self worth. I was as good as any of the cadre or officers; in no way did their rank make them better than I. It gave them power and authority over me but that did not make them better. I would play their game since there was no sense asking for trouble. But every chance I got, I would kick against the pricks designed to break me down. When I was going through the turmoil of the teen years, I often had feelings of worthlessness, often lacked positive feelings of self-esteem. It was at this time that my mother would tell me, "Don't ever forget you are a child of God, and as such you are a person of great worth. Don't ever let anyone put you down, always hold your head up high." That was sage advice and stood me in good stead, not only when the constant drum beat in the Army attempted to pull me down, but at other times in my life when I felt my self esteem slipping. My mother was a gem.

WILL THE REAL ENEMY
PLEASE STEP FORWARD

"Korea, Land of the Morning Calm. I have heard so much about it and now, here I am, standing on the deck of the ship looking at it. At the moment, it certainly doesn't appear very calm." These are the words I used to open the brief letter penned to Bonnie on the morning of March 12, 1953. (Unless indicated otherwise, from this point on, all quotes are lifted directly from the letters sent to Bonnie.)

Since Inchon has no natural harbor, the the ship anchored two or three miles from the shore on the morning of March 12. It would be necessary to make an amphibious landing. As soon as the ship anchored, all troops were herded to the top deck where we stood cramped like sardines while the steel platform we would walk on to reach the landing craft was laid on the water. That was something to watch. I certainly had no idea that large sheets of steel laid on the water would float but when all were connected, float they did. There must have been tons and tons of steel that not only floated, but also supported the weight of the troops as we disembarked from the ship onto the steel platform. I could hear artillery fire and saw numerous planes sliding in and out of the Inchon area. We had been told nothing so I assumed the enemy was just over the first row of hills. And, of course, the military did all it could to foster that assumption. While standing on deck, I had a good chance to look around. There were various ships anchored about, including a large hospital ship. I never did find out just what kind of casualties were evacuated to the hospital ship. The troop ship was the only ship that would be discharging troops on March 12.

It was early evening before the first landing craft began ferrying troops from the ship to the beach. There were approximately 4,000 men on the ship and it was dark before all troops had been transported to shore. In fact, it was dark before I boarded the landing craft and made the very cold trip to shore. The only thing we were told was to be very, very quiet and to proceed immediately to a train, which was parked a short distance from the landing site. It was a very dark night and there were no lights in the cars of the train. Neither was there any heat.

Once we were loaded on the train, an officer stepped inside and picked a man to step outside to keep watch each time the train stopped. Supposedly this was done in case the enemy made an attack upon the train. Small difference that one guard would have made. The illusion that the enemy was close by was maintained. The only thing the officer said to the troops was that the train would take us to Yongdung P'o, the replacement depot for divisions on line. While at Camp Drake, outside of Yokohama, I had been assigned to the Clearing Company, 120th Medical Battalion, 45th Infantry Division, perhaps better known as the Thunderbirds. I would be going to the 45th Infantry Division Replacement Depot. The 45th Division is an Oklahoma National Guard Division and entered the war from Hokkaido, Japan, in December of 1951.

It took a few hours to reach Yongdung P'o, though in actual miles it really wasn't that far. Korea is a peninsula only about 100 miles wide. Inchon is on the west coast so we had to go east to reach Yongdung P'o. It was the frequent stops of the train and the snail's pace at which it proceeded that made the short journey seem so long. The trip was made without incident.

Once at Yongdung P'o, processing began immediately and went on until 3:30 a.m. In addition to maintaining the illusion that the enemy was just over the hill, the illusion was created that great haste was necessary to get replacements to their respective units. In reality, the Chinese troops were many miles from Yongdung P'o and from Inchon. In addition, there was no need for haste other than to empty the replacement depot of men in order to get ready for the next shipload. When I did arrive at Clearing Company, it was days before I started functioning as a medic. Until then I was assigned to a work detail, moving sand from one place to another and then back again.

Most of the processing involved the issuing of additional cold weather clothing; heavy field pants, field jacket liner, heavy wool shirts, parka with a fur lined hood, rabbit most likely. In addition there were thermo boots which were affectionately referred to as "Mickey Mouse Boots" because they resembled the feet of Mickey Mouse, helmet liner, mess kit, canteen, entrenching tool and shelter half. Yes, I was issued only half of a pup tent or shelter; some other fellow got the other half.

Though it was short, the time in Yongdung P'o gave me a chance to see some of the ravages of war. Yongdung P'o, at the time, was a suburb of Seoul. As far as one could see, hardly a building had been left standing. If the goal of the North Koreans was to destroy Seoul, from my perspective at least, they were successful. What impressed me most was the number of small children hanging around the periphery of the replacement depot. Most of the children were dressed in what would best be described as summer attire. The children looked as if they were on the verge of starvation. I was told later that most of these children had been orphaned when first the North Koreans and then the Chinese swept through Seoul some two and one half years earlier.

One morning I was walking around the depot area when I saw a strange looking, oxen driven vehicle enter the compound. The vehicle had small front wheels but very large rear wheels. The Korean driver immediately pulled his cart behind the nearest latrine, opened a hinged door at the back and commenced shoveling the contents into his cart. When he was finished, he went to the next latrine, then the next until he had emptied all of the enlisted men's latrines of their contents. Next he pulled his cart or wagon behind the officer's latrine and commenced shoveling the waste out of it into his wagon. That wagon, by the way was euphemistically referred to as a "honey wagon." The connection was not lost on the thinking person. I found this most interesting and wondered what he was going to do with all that human waste. I asked one of the men who was stationed at the replacement depot and he informed me that Koreans use human waste to fertilize their rice paddies and this was a routine that went on every morning. My naivete' was showing; I should have known. With a smile on my face, I asked him if the old fellow had to pay more for the officer's crap than for that of the enlisted men…"Naw," was his reply, "he gets it for nothing." I had already assumed that much in spite of my naivete'.

Here comes the Honey Wagon

The children hanging around the periphery of the compound were especially noticeable during mealtime. The compound was encircled with rolled barbed wire, however, I noticed several small holes in the wire in the vicinity of the garbage cans. The first morning I was at the depot, after breakfast I walked out the door of the mess hall and headed for the garbage cans. I didn't get very far when a very small boy wriggled through the hole in the barbed wire, made a beeline for me and very deftly scooped the remaining food on my tray into a gallon bucket he was carrying. After finishing with me, he moved to the next fellow and the next until his gallon was filled with slop and then he made a dash for the hole in the fence, slithered through and immediately commenced filling his little hand with the slop and shoving it into his mouth.

One little boy was not so fortunate. After filling his bucket with garbage from one of the garbage cans, garbage consisting of a mixture of oatmeal, eggs, toast, pancakes, and potatoes awash in cold coffee, he started back towards the fence. It may have been garbage to those tending the cans, but it was life-sustaining food to the children. Suddenly, one of the men on K.P. dashed out of the kitchen, caught up with the little fellow, and planted a solid kick on his butt, sending him and his slop bucket flying through the air. The poor little guy cried out in terror. Leaving his can on the ground, he scurried as quickly as he could through the hole in the fence.

Watching that sorry display was an old sergeant. Not really old but when one is 22, even 40 is old. As the fellow on K.P. started back to the kitchen, the sergeant intercepted him, grabbed him by the front of his jacket and pulled him to his face. "So help me," he said, "If I ever see you doing that again, I am going to knock the hell out of you." The fellow mumbled something about garbage, bad alcohol, G.Is. dying, etc. The sergeant let him go and he went back into the kitchen. Apparently the old sarge felt some kind of explanation was in order, and he proceeded to tell us gathered about him that he saw so many starving children in Europe following World War II that he could no longer bear to see hungry children. He also reminded us that the slop in the garbage cans, like the crap from the latrines, ended up on some farmer's rice paddies. "And they would keep the children from eating it?" he asked. "I don't understand this damn Army."

"You will never believe what I saw this evening. In fact, I am still in a state of disbelief. Never for a moment would I have believed that the enemy was small children."

Children will be children no matter where they are (Ch'unch'on)

It was the last evening I was in Yongdung P'o. Supper was behind me and I was outside watching the children in the field adjacent to the mess hall. They had to be cold, dressed so scantily. I couldn't help but feel guilty what with all of the cold weather gear piled on my body. I found myself hoping they would survive the cold until spring and warmer weather arrived, which really wasn't that far away. Suddenly three jeeps filled with M.Ps. came tearing into the compound, drove up to the barbed wire fence and stopped. The M.Ps., armed with M.l. Carbines, jumped out of the jeeps and immediately started shooting in the direction of the children. I was dumb founded. I could not believe what I was seeing and hearing. Of course, they were not shooting to hit the children, but some of those bullets were striking very close. In addition, the ground was still frozen and there was nothing to keep those bullets from ricocheting. To say the least, it was a very dangerous situation for the children who ran screaming from the fence. The firing continued until the field adjacent to the mess hall was cleared of children. And beyond the field were adults, many adults who witnessed this whole sorry spectacle. Is this why I was sent to Korea, to watch American G.Is. shooting at children? Just who was the enemy anyway? Children wanting only to get a meal from garbage cans or the fellows in the trenches a good many miles to the north? I was confused. I was angry. At that moment, I felt chagrined to be wearing the American uniform. I needed an explanation and I needed clarification, which, of course, I never got. Will the real enemy please step forward?

On March 15th orders came through for me to be transported to the Clearing Company, 120th Medical Battalion, 45th Infantry Division. I can't say I was sorry to leave Yongdung P'o. The memories of that place were not pleasant, and it took some time for me to get over the shock of seeing American G.Is. emptying their carbines at helpless little children scared to death of being shot. In fact, to this day, that incident leaves a bitter taste in my mouth.

A Clearing Company is just that, a clearing company. Each Regiment, the 179th, the 180th, and the 279th, had a medical aid station. At the aid station, if necessary, life saving procedures were undertaken after which the casualty was brought by ambulance to Clearing Company. In addition to battle casualties, men from the regiments on sick call and those who couldn't be treated at the aid station were also brought to Clearing Company. If a wound was slight, something that would largely heal in a week or 10 days, the casualty was kept at Clearing Company and then returned to duty. The same thing was true of men on sick call. If their illnesses were not serious, they were kept a few days and then returned to their unit. However, if the wound or illness were serious, then the doctors would make a decision to have the individual transferred either by ambulance or helicopter, to a Mobile Army Surgical Hospital (MASH), Army Surgical Hospital (ASH), or the 121st Evacuation Hospital in Seoul. In effect, then, Clearing Company was a sorting station, sorting out men from the Division, wounded or ill, with the doctors making the decision who should stay and who should be evacuated or transferred. At Clearing Company, shortly after arriving, I was assigned two duties: l) as a medic in the Emergency Wing of the hospital and 2) later as an Admissions and

Disposition Clerk since I was one of the very few men in the Company who could type. Since reports had to be made up in the evening, I worked in E.R. during the day and typed the daily reports around 8:00 p.m. every evening.

With orders in hand, almost immediately I boarded a truck for the short ride to the train depot in Seoul. Seoul was ravaged. Most buildings were seriously damaged or completely destroyed from artillery attacks and bombs. I had a chance to see the capital building. It was a mere skeleton. All the windows were gone and the inside had been gutted by fire. Small wonder that Seoul was so devastated since it had been fought over twice. The first time was when North Korea invaded the South and the second time was when the Chinese entered the war. Once the truck reached the train depot or what was left of it, I boarded a train for Ch'unch'on and the 45th Infantry Division School of Standards. At this time the 45th Division was on line covering such notorious places as The Punchbowl, Sandbag Castle, Heartbreak Ridge, etc, located near previously occupied villages with names like Hwach'on, Yanggu, Inje, etc. While at the depot waiting for the train to move, I saw yet another most pathetic sight. There were small children everywhere trying to sell trinkets, most made of brass from shell casings scavenged from training areas. Like the children at Yongdung P'o, they were far from adequately dressed, and it was cold, darn cold. It was cloudy and a light snow was coming down. One little boy stands out in my mind. He was wearing only a short little jacket. He had no trousers, no underclothing. His little body, from the waist on down was blue from the cold; his feet were bare. He came to up to the train window and stood looking at me for a handout. I was going to give him a pair of wool socks, which were at the bottom of my duffel bag. It was against regulations to help these children in any way. But damned be the regulations, the little fellow was freezing to death. I started rummaging through the bag,but before I got to the socks, the train was moving and soon the small boy was out of sight. I felt that somehow I had failed him though I don't know what good one pair of socks would have done. I felt so helpless; there was nothing I could do to save that little boy's life. To the world he was only a cipher, but to me he was a small human being desperately in need of help and there was no one who would step forward to do so. Like the hungry children at Yongdung P'o, I have never been able to get that pathetic little figure out of my mind. I can still see that shivering little body, and those eyes, those eyes pleading for help. My God in heaven, why the children?

GREATER LOVE HAS NO MAN

His name was Stanley Crooks. There was nothing distinguishing about Stanley, he was not the kind of person who would stand out in a crowd. I remember him as being rather short of stature and very quiet in disposition. Stanley came to Clearing Company, 120th Medical Battalion, about one month after I arrived. By religious faith he was a 7th Day Adventist. Now Adventists almost always applied for and were granted non-combatant status. The phrase "non-combatant" needs to be clarified. Most non-initiates believe it means that the person so classified will never be assigned to a combat zone or unit. That is wrong, totally wrong. That is not the case at all. What it meant, in Korea at least, was that when a non-combatant was assigned to a combat zone, he would not be required to carry a weapon. It was for this reason that those classified as IAO, non-combatants or conscientious objectors, were almost always assigned to the medics. Seventh Day Adventists, along with many others classified as non-combatants, believed it was wrong to kill in war, however, they would accept assignment to a medical unit where they would be able to do something constructive rather than destructive. I have no idea how many men in the medics were non-combatants. Suffice it to say, many. For the military this caused a problem since every man who refused to carry a weapon decreased the firepower of the unit, medical or otherwise.

Stanley was a tent mate and I got to know him well. He and I had a lot in common. Both of us were the same age, both of us gave our sweethearts a diamond before shipping out for Korea, both of us lived for that day when we would be returning to the states, to the girl of our dreams, to marriage and to starting a family. We would talk often about our hopes and aspirations. Of course, always in the back of our minds was the very real possibility that we would not be able to realize any of those hopes and aspirations, ever. We tended, as much as possible, to push those thoughts to the back of our minds.

One day a rumor started circulating that there were too many non-combatants assigned to Clearing Company, 120th Medical Battalion, and that some would be singled out to be transferred to the regiments to become "line" medics. The rumor was not new; it would surface from time to time so we didn't give too much thought to it. However, within a few days, orders were cut for a few of the men to be transferred, not all of them non-combatants. One of those receiving such orders was Stanley Crooks. All of us who knew Stanley, hated to see him go, however, he was philosophical about it and the coming transfer didn't seem to cause him much concern. Stanley was a person of deep spiritual faith and this undoubtedly played no small part in what could only be called a positive outlook. In a few days Stanley's orders were cut, a jeep from the 279th Infantry Regiment arrived to transport him to the front lines, we said our good byes, and Stanley was gone.

As in any organization one has to have friends. In the military, in a combat situation, friendships are often short lived since the status of people is constantly changing. Some are transferred to other units, some rotate home, some are killed. It is always risky to form friendships that are too emotionally close since they can be terminated abruptly. I missed Stanley and I missed our frequent conversations. From time-to-time he would come to Clearing Company with an ambulance containing battle casualties and men reporting in on sick call. On these occasions, we would go to the mess hall and visit over a cup of coffee and the cook's famous string thin raised donuts. On one occasion I asked Stanley how it was up at regimental aid station. "You know, Dick," he replied, "it's really not so bad. I don't mind it at all."

Shortly after his arrival at the front, Stanley was awarded the Silver Star for heroism. Now Silver Stars are not handed out to just anyone. I never did find out what he did to receive that most prestigious award. In fact, had I asked him, I'm sure he would not have revealed the real reason anyway. That's the kind of person Stanley was.

The workday was divided into shifts. Those working the night shift put in a 14 hour shift while those working days put in a 10 hour shift. Although there were times when the nights got very busy, most of the casualties and all but emergency sick call patients came in during the day. Although shifts rotated, at this time I was working the day shift. Stanley had been gone for some time and those of us who considered him a friend had gotten used to his absence. The fact that he rather enjoyed his duties at the 279th aid station made his absence easier to take.

"This morning when I got to work, there was a rumor circulating that Stanley Crooks had been killed during the night. So far it's only a rumor and even that is totally lacking in detail. By 10:00 we will know more and by the time I seal this letter this evening, the rumor will either have been confirmed or revealed as just that, a rumor. I will keep you posted." On July 6th, I was working the day shift, which meant my workday started at 8:00 a.m. When I walked into the E.R. (emergency room), I was told that someone had heard that Stanley Crooks had been killed during the night. I was in disbelief. There had to be a mistake. Perhaps there was another Stanley Crooks; perhaps someone had made a typographical error. It would be 10:00 before the regimental casualty lists for the night would be received at Clearing Company. Those two hours seemed an eternity. At 10:00, the division casualty list was received. As I scanned the list, there it was. It was no error. In bold black against white, listed under K.I.A. (killed in action) was the name, Stanley Crooks, with his accompanying rank and serial number. I was in a state of shock. It was no rumor. It was no mistake after all. Stanley was dead and with him died all of his plans, his aspirations, his future. There was a young woman in Kansas, who would not be getting married to Stanley Crooks during the summer of 1954. A plethora of questions raced through my mind: Why Stanley? How come he was chosen to go to the 279th as a line medic? How come it wasn't I? It could just as easily have been. Why not Stanley? There were other men whose names were listed under K.I.A. (Killed in Action). When losing a close friend, one is not always the most rational.

The night Stanley was killed another line medic from the 279th was wounded. I was told his wounds were not serious and that he was on one of the hospital wards. As soon as I could, I went to see him with that burning question on my mind: how did it happen? How did Stan get killed? During the night Stan's unit came under heavy enemy artillery fire. A G.I. from Stan's outfit was a bit forward of the trench when he was struck by shrapnel. Not only was he calling for help, but he was calling for Stanley by name. However, the artillery attack was so intense that Stan's commanding officer ordered him to stay within the relative safety of the trench. Stan's response was that one of his men was wounded out there, and he had to see if he could help him. In effect, he disobeyed an order, left the trench and inched his way toward the voice of the wounded man. Stan reached the man and administered first aid. The man had lost a considerable amount of blood and was in need of plasma. Stan got the man to a nearby sand bag bunker when an incoming round made a direct hit on the bunker killing Stan and the other man instantly. The wounded medic asked, "Why did he do something like that. Why did he place his life in danger when he didn't have to?" Indeed, Stan would not have had to leave the relative safety of the trench, but knowing Stan he could not crouch in a trench when one of his men needed him so desperately. And so, not having to do so, he gave his life in an effort to save that of a friend. In contemplating his own death, Jesus said, "Greater love has no man than this, that a man lay down his life for his friends." (The Bible, KJV, John 15, Vs 13) I have no doubt that when Stan was ushered into the presence of his Maker, he was greeted with the words, "Well done good and faithful servant."

His name was Stanley Crooks. There was nothing distinguishing about him. He was not the kind of person who would stand out in a crowd. He was quiet and rather short of stature. But inside, Stanley Crooks was a giant of a man.

A CASUALTY OF WAR

The conceptualization of post traumatic shock syndrome, following the Vietnam War, reminded us that not all the scars of war are permanently etched into the body. For many, the scar is etched into the mind. Undoubtedly for some, the trauma inflicted on the mind by an incident of war can be as great as and even greater than the trauma inflicted upon the body by a bullet or flying shrapnel.

It had been an extremely heavy night so far as casualties were concerned. They just didn't stop coming. Most were serious wounds and the casualties were either evacuated to the 121st Evac in Seoul by helicopter or to a close by ASH or MASH hospital by ambulance.

Clearing Company, 120ᵗʰ Medical Battalion. Location When I First Arrived in Korea

Toward the end of the day, yet another ambulance loaded with casualties drove into the compound. Among the wounded were two men from the same tank crew. One had suffered a rather severe wound from rifle fire; the other was a walking wounded. It was obvious the two men were buddies. It was necessary for me to find out how each man was wounded so I started asking questions of the man who lay on the stretcher. I couldn't get any response out of him. He just lay there not moving, staring off into space and seemingly oblivious of my questions. I tried with my questions a couple of times, but he only remained silent and unmoving. Finally, I turned to his buddy and asked, "Can you tell me what happened?" "Sure," was his reply. In addition to giving me the man's name, rank and serial number, he proceeded to tell me the following.

The two men were members of a tank crew located on a jutting finger of land where the M.L.R. (main line of resistance) or front line took a sharp turn in the direction of enemy lines. I can't recall how many men made up a tank crew; however, these men were gathered by the side of the tank eating their evening meal. In so far as was possible, the men on the front line were fed one hot meal a day. Generally this was the evening meal, which was flown in by helicopter. Meal time varied since, through one means or another, the enemy very often discovered the time that the meal on a particular day would be served, waited until the men were standing in line to receive their dinner, and then poured in rounds of artillery, often wounding and/or killing several men and always demoralizing them. As the tank crew was eating their evening meal, unknown to them, a number of enemy soldiers had worked their way into the trench beside the parked tank and were approaching the men gathered by the side of the tank. Without any kind of warning the enemy opened fire, killing one of the men and wounding a couple more. Now the man who was killed was a new replacement having arrived at the tank site just a few hours earlier. The man on the stretcher had been wounded in the initial burst of enemy fire, but not badly enough to put him down. Very often tank crews were issued M3 sub machine guns since it was short and more maneuverable inside a crowded tank. The M3 was affectionately at times and not so affectionately at others referred to as a "grease gun," since in appearance that is what it looked like. The M3 was a very effective close range weapon in 45 caliber. If my memory serves me correctly, some that I saw had no rifling in the barrel, making them especially deadly since the bullets would exit the barrel in a tumbling manner called key holeing. To say the least, to be struck by one of those tumbling 230 grain bullets would cause a very nasty wound. In spite of the fact he was wounded, the man on the stretcher grabbed his grease gun, jumped into the trench, and opened fire on the enemy soldiers. Now the magazine of the M3 held 30 rounds, making it even more formidable. He continued firing until every one of the enemy soldiers lay dead at his feet. That "every one" added up to seven men. He then lifted himself out of the trench, lay down and from that point on, did not utter another word. The buddy who was relating the incident to me said that it was the death of the new replacement that so incensed the man that he forsook his own wounds and safety and went after the enemy soldiers. However, when the enormity of the number of men he had killed sunk in, he became silent, almost, it appeared, assuming a catatonic state. During the time it took the buddy to tell me what happened, the soldier on the stretcher had not moved nor had his eyes changed from that unblinking stare. He would be deemed a hero, of course, however, he was also a casualty of war, suffering both wounds to his body and his mind. It is not unreasonable to assume that whereas the wounds to his body healed rather quickly, the wounds to his mind healed slowly if, indeed, healing ever did take place.

It is not easy for the military to take a young man raised in a culture that believes the taking of another human life is one of the foulest deeds committed and make a successful killer out of him. Yet that is exactly what the military tries to do and only with some success. A number of studies revealed that during the Korean War in any single firefight when the enemy was engaged less that 50 percent of the American boys used their weapons. This in spite of the fact that they were being fired upon and their

.lives were in jeopardy. The problem is that after 18 or 20 years of socialization into such a high intensity value as the sanctity of human life, the resocialization the military attempted in just eight weeks, for many, many men, at least, was ineffective. The military may not have liked it, but the fact does say something about the effectiveness of our earlier and later socialization into the value and belief system of American culture. Some may disagree. My response is to say, check the record; it is available. In particular look at some of the work of General S.L.A.M. Marshall.

One of the ways the military attempted to overcome the effects of 18 or 20 years of socialization was to do their best to dehumanize the enemy. The hope was that by so doing, it would be easier to kill. And so, the North Koreans and Chinese became Gooks, not men nor human beings, but Gooks. "You aren't killing humans, you are killing Gooks." And, to a degree, I'm sure, it worked. This was done during World War II and I believe it was done most effectively. How well I recall making the drive between Freeman and Sioux Falls and seeing huge road signs depicting the Japanese not as human beings, but as rats dressed in a Japanese military uniform. These signs were not for the consumption of military men but for the American populace in general. But for many of the troops, there came a time when the efforts to dehumanize the enemy wore thin. Troops realized that the enemy wasn't fighting to make the world a safer place for, in their case Communism. They were fighting just to keep alive. In short, the enemy was very much like them, drafted into a war they didn't want to fight and hoping against hope that they would survive it in order to return to family and home.

There was at Clearing Company, 120th Medical Battalion, a Master Sergeant, a career man who was up at the Chosin Reservoir with the 1st Cavalry, when the Chinese attacked. A half million Chinese troops had crossed the river, and when they attacked U.S. forces, 300,000 men were thrown into the battle. In conversation with him one day, he told me that although the military attempted to portray the retreat from the Yalu as an orderly withdrawal of troops, it was a rout. It was every man for himself.

At one point he found himself in a bunker with a satchel full of hand grenades. Chinese soldiers were flowing by his bunker like so much water; they were everywhere. He told me that he would take a grenade, pull the pin, hold the handle until no Chinese were in sight, and then let it roll downhill from the bunker. He looked at me and said, "Even though my life was hanging by a thread, Waltner, I could not kill anyone, not a North Korean, not a Chinese, no one and so, I made sure my grenades would roll down the hill and explode harmlessly, not hurting or killing anyone." To be sure, there were others who told me similar stories. Of course, on the other hand, there were men who became very efficient killers and, it would appear, enjoyed doing so. I will touch on this in a later chapter.

And so the young man on the stretcher was immobilized by the realization that in a moment of anger and, I suppose, hatred, he had killed seven men, men who were just doing their job like he was doing his. That knowledge is something he would have to live with for the rest of his life. I would say he was a perfect candidate for post traumatic shock syndrome even though it would be another 15 or 20 years before that emotional, psychological syndrome or pattern would even be conceptualized.

MEN DON'T CRY

It is something American males have drummed into them from early childhood on: men don't cry. The little girl on the playground can injure herself and run crying to the teacher. She is comforted with the words; "There, there dear, its all right. You have a good cry and pretty soon the owey will go away." But the little boy who injures himself on the playground and runs to the teacher for solace and comfort is most likely to hear, "Now be a big boy and don't cry. It's really not that bad." Don't cry, don't cry, don't cry. It goes on and on and in time it becomes almost impossible to cry. During football practice one day back in 1947, one of the players got knocked to the ground. Someone stepped on his face with a cleat on either side of his nose and a turning foot instantly broke the fellow's nose. Immediately he cried out and writhed on the ground in pain, moaning and groaning. The coach ran over to him, lifted him to his feet by the back of his jersey and said, "No player of mine is going to be a cry baby when he gets a little bit hurt." And with that, he gave him a quick kick in the butt that sent him sprawling on the ground. Boys don't cry, men don't cry. When first my father and then my mother died in rather quick succession, I cried, two of the few times I have cried that I can remember. However, as with crying at the death of my daughter, I did my crying in the shower again, not wanting my wife to see my "weakness" revealed. Men don't cry even when they have every reason to cry.

Women's Liberation was supposed to do away with this double standard, this stereotype. I believe the movement failed miserably in doing so. The message is still clear, men don't cry. On several occasions I polled female students in my sociology classes. I found little support or sympathy for a crying male. Some of the responses were, "I would feel very

38

uncomfortable in the presence of a male who was crying," "I wouldn't know what to do or say," "I would feel very insecure if my boyfriend cried," etc., etc. Now, this was just a few short years ago well after the women's liberation movement promised, yes promised, that men as well as women would be liberated. Liberated from what? Certainly they would not be liberated from the proscription against crying. Men don't cry and if they do they are likely to be rejected even though it is now known that a good cry can be psychologically healthy. Men don't cry because if they did their male peers would ridicule them, and their female friends would consider them less than masculine and might well abandon them. What a heavy burden culture has imposed on men by denying them the right to cry when Lord knows, they are entitled to do so.

Private Green was brought in by ambulance around 8:00 p.m. one evening in May. He had just finished his evening meal and was crawling back into his foxhole when a sniper shot him. The bullet went through both upper thighs and just grazed his scrotum. Had that bullet been one inch higher, it would have destroyed his testicles. The fighting along the entire front had intensified. One consequence was that casualties that we ordinarily would have sent back to an ASH or a MASH had to be treated by our doctors. A Clearing Company is not equipped to handle major surgery, but in this case we had no choice. With wounds like Private Green suffered, major surgery would be required. A deep incision would have to be made at both the bullet's entry and exit sites. And all we had to anesthesia him with was a local anesthetic, novacaine. Yes, the same novacaine the dentist uses to deaden your mouth when working on your teeth. The doctors used plenty of novacaine, but when they started using the scalpel to make the incisions, it was obvious from Private Green's reaction that he felt the cut of the knife. Throughout most of the surgery, Private Green quivered in pain. Dr. Bradford, the doctor working on Private Green, was livid with anger, angry that he had to perform such surgery with nothing more than novacaine to dull the pain. Of course, Green was conscious during the entire ordeal. At one point Dr. Bradshaw engaged him in conversation, more to get the Private's mind off the surgery than to gain information. However, when Green said that he had a bachelor's degree, Dr. Bradford came unglued. "What in the hell are you doing up on the front lines?" he asked. "With four years of college, the Army certainly has a place for you in a rear echelon outfit." It is obvious the good doctor knew nothing about men in skirts.

Once the incisions were made, a rubber drain was forced through the incision and the hole made by the bullet so the channel that had been formed could be cleansed. Now imagine if you will, a hole through both of your upper thighs with the two ends of a rubber drain dangling outside the wounds on both legs. When both legs had been debrided and sterilized, Dr. Bradford used more novacaine and sutured the wounds. When he finished with the legs, he turned his attention to Private Green's scrotum, which had what looked like a deep burn across the bottom. Without so much as novacaine, the doctor took his scalpel and slowly cut away the dead skin. Finally, Dr. Bradshaw was finished and Private Green was taken to one of the wards. From the moment he arrived in the E.R. until he was placed in the ward, Private Green didn't so much as make a peep. You see, men don't cry even when they have a darn good reason to do so.

On another occasion, a Warrant Officer was also brought in by ambulance. He had caught a rather large piece of shrapnel in his left buttock. It was in so deep that it lay up against his pelvic bone. Again, it was a wound that needed the facilities of a MASH or ASH unit. Accordingly, he was sent to the closest ASH some miles down the road. However, just as when Private Green was wounded, there was much activity up front and ASH was swamped with casualties. The ambulance brought the Warrant Officer back to Clearing Company with instructions from ASH doctors to "Do the best you can." He was taken into surgery, and using the omnipresent novacaine the doctor went to work. First he shot the wound full of novacaine to provide at least a little deadening. Next he took a probe and inserted it into the wound made by the shrapnel. He found it and also discovered that the shrapnel was deeply imbedded. He would have to make a deep incision in order to extricate the shrapnel. This he did. It was obvious the Warrant Officer was in much pain. Finally with much probing and pushing and tugging, the piece of shrapnel was removed. During the probing and tugging on the shrapnel, the pain was so intense at one point that the Warrant Officer moved his head over to the side of the operating table and vomited on the floor. This absolutely humiliated him, and I recall how he apologized again and again for not being able to take the pain. That's right, he apologized for vomiting when he was undergoing surgery that should have been performed under general anesthesia. Like Private Green, he never so much as let out a single cry, but he vomited. A real he man takes the pain, he doesn't cry out, he doesn't whimper, he doesn't vomit and above all, he never, never cries even when he has the best of reasons to do so. You see, men don't cry.

A Miracle in the Emergency Room

"Early this morning, I witnessed a miracle in the emergency room. I don't know what else to call it. I have thought much about what transpired and no other word or words will suffice. Just to be there was a thrilling experience. I felt a sense of elation throughout the day. I don't know what the other men felt, for I didn't discuss it with them. But from the atmosphere in the E.R., I am positive all of us, including Dr. Shearer, felt and experienced something far different from what we have when working on other casualties."

Everyone or almost everyone has heard of battlefield miracles. Undoubtedly some of them were indeed miracles. Others may not have been miracles but reflected the skill of the attending physician and/or medical team, but as such, most likely would not be called miracles. I was rather skeptical myself until I was a participant in what I would call a true battlefield miracle. Others may disagree and that is fine with me. Forty-seven years later and with much, much thought given to that experience, my conclusion is still the same. Lieutenant Drackman's life was saved by the grace of God. Of course, we, all of us who worked on the Lieutenant, assisted in his survival. But without the presence of God in that E.R., I am convinced the Lieutenant would have died. And that is exactly what it was, a presence, an unexplainable presence that was so real it was almost palpable. And this is coming from one who was trained as a social scientist, an empiricist, but also one who has learned that there is more to this world and to life than empiricism. There is also a non-empirical realm, and it is found in beliefs, values and norms to name just a few examples.

The time was late May and after a couple of slow starts, spring was definitely in the air. Korea was no different from any other country, which has seasons, divided into fall, winter, spring and summer. After a long and cold winter and a late spring characterized by rain, snow, more rain, mud, and more snow, the mountains were beginning to turn green. Even in our earthen compound, a few tufts of green grass, maybe weeds, were beginning to show. In addition, the mornings and evenings were lengthening considerably. It was now possible to stay outdoors longer in the evening and start the day outdoors earlier in the a.m. When one is young, spring is a wonderful time of the year. Even though death was a daily occurrence, it was hard to think of death. It was easier to think of love and romance, of the coming warm temperatures, of rain and nights filled with the color purple. Everything was coming alive and it was easy to get in tune with this symphony.

At this time, I was working the night shift. The hour must have been about 4:30 a.m. Just after the dark of night began to lift, I heard a cuckoo. Yes, there are cuckoo birds in Korea but, though I heard them on occasion, I had yet to see one. I was curious about the appearance of the bird. I had been told it was a rather large bird, about the size of a pigeon. Quietly I opened the door to the E.R. and slipped outside. We were in the mountains and the air was still quite chilly. Slowly I walked towards the place from which the sound of the bird appeared to be coming. Sure enough, there sitting on a stump (there were no trees left standing) of a tree was this rather large bird singing to its heart's content. I had seen a cuckoo and I felt good about it.

As I turned to go back to the E.R., I heard the high-pitched whine of a vehicle coming down off the hill. Clearing Company was located at the bottom of that long, steep, winding road that ascended and descended a mountain. The vehicle, which turned out to be a litter jeep, was geared down to minimize use of the brakes and to keep the vehicle from going too fast. I stopped and waited. In short order, the litter jeep pulled into the compound. I directed the driver to pull up close to the doors of the E.R. There were three people in the jeep: the driver, a medic and a casualty in a litter, which was secured sideways in the back of the jeep. I walked over to the jeep, took a look at the man in the litter, and thought he was dead. His pallor had the look of death about it, sort of a slate gray color. His eyes were closed and he was lying very still. I ran to the E.R., jerked open the door and called for help. We lifted the litter from the jeep and in setting it on the ground tipped it slightly sideways. Immediately a heavy stream of blood flowed from the litter. The only visible wound on the man's body was a leg wound, which the medics at the artillery outfit had treated well. There was no blood coming from the bandaged leg. There had to be another wound that the medics up front had over looked. It was obvious we would have to work fast if the man's life was to be saved.

We removed the man from the bloody stretcher onto one from the E.R. and while two medics carried him into the E.R., another medic and I carried the blood filled litter to a small bridge, which crossed a small stream flowing through the compound. We upended the litter and let the blood drain into the water. For a moment, it ran crimson red. Dr. Shearer was on duty. Immediately upon the wounded man's arrival in the compound, one of the medics ran to his tent to awaken him. In just a few moments Dr. Shearer arrived. Now Dr. Shearer was an older man, a man in his mid to later thirties, a man who had plenty of experience before ever coming to Korea. He took one look at Lieutenant Drackman and shouted, "Get some blood into this man." We tried but we couldn't. The Lieutenant had lost so much blood that his veins had collapsed.

Now it so happened that at this time, the Division Chaplain had a small Quonset hut at Clearing Company; the current chaplain was Catholic. The occupancy of the Quonset would often change. From a Catholic chaplain to a Protestant chaplain and then back again to a Catholic chaplain, etc. Father Benson, early on, had left word that any time a casualty was brought into the E.R. he was to be called immediately. This time there was a sense of urgency about it, and within moments he was at the side of Lt. Drackman. We explained the situation to him; the Lieutenant had lost most of his blood and we couldn't get any blood into his body. His vital signs? There were none, no discernable pulse, blood pressure or respiration. The Lieutenant's situation was extremely grave and he was dying. Most amazing was that the Lieutenant was conscious. He shouldn't have been. I was at the head of the litter when Father Benson bent his head close to that of Lt. Drackman. "My son," he said, "I am going back to my quarters and I am going to pray for you." Lt Drackman opened his eyes ever so slightly and gazed into Father Benson's face and replied very faintly, "Father, I am not a Catholic." (Father Benson had a crucifix dangling from his neck). Father Benson's response was, "It makes no difference if you are a Catholic or not, I am going to go and pray for you." Father Benson left orders that unless death appeared imminent he was not to be disturbed. He then left the E.R. and went to his Quonset.

By this time we were frantic. There was no way the Lieutenant could last much longer if we didn't get blood into him and get it into him fast. In fact, it was a miracle he was still living. Dr. Shearer said quite simply, "We are going to have to force blood into his body." With that, he grabbed a scalpel and with deft cuts exposed major veins in both wrists and both ankles. I watched as he made these incisions. What impressed me was that there was no bleeding. He quickly rigged a needle and tube with a bulb attached. Try as I may, I can't remember what it looked like and I wish I could. With a needle inserted in a vein in both ankles and both wrists and with a container of blood hanging over each appendage, we slowly started pumping blood into Lt. Drackman's body. That morning in the E.R., I witnessed a miracle.

As we started slowly pumping the blood into the Lieutenant's body, a hush came over the room. No one talked but everyone performed his task flawlessly without having to be reminded by Dr. Shearer what to do. We worked on Lt. Drackman for several hours. Slowly his vital signs began to manifest themselves, his blood pressure, his pulse and his respirations. I do believe that not only Father Benson, but all of us we were praying for the Lieutenant. All of us had worked as a medical team with Dr. Shearer before on other casualties, but this was different. Dr. Shearer and team functioned like a precision timepiece. Very few words were spoken; they didn't have to be. Each medic performed his roles flawlessly...

The jeep carrying Lt. Drackman pulled into the compound around 4:30 a.m. It was around 8:00 a.m. when Dr. Shearer announced that the Lieutenant was now out of danger. By the grace of God, Lt. Drackman's life had been spared. Inwardly I shed a few tears, as I am sure the others did. It would seem that a kind of bonding had taken place between the Lieutenant and those of us on duty that early morning. When the Lieutenant was out of danger, one of the medics went to get Father Benson. When he came into the E.R. and saw the lieutenant's pallor, which was now normal, I could see the tension drain from his face.

Where had all that blood in the litter come from? Lt. Drackman's most obvious wound was a badly injured leg. This was treated as well as could be expected given the supplies, etc. available at the aid station. However, the medics had over looked a small hole in the Lieutenant's left axillary area where a piece of shrapnel had entered. That piece of shrapnel had pierced the Lieutenant's left lung and had caused the almost fatal loss of blood.

Lieutenant Drackman was the commanding officer of an artillery unit. The unit had been struck by an artillery attack launched by the enemy. A hit was made on one of the sand bag bunkers and one of the men was wounded. Another of the men in the bunker quickly got Lt. Drackman, who immediately went to the bunker to see how badly wounded the man was. Just after he entered the bunker came the sound of another incoming round. Lt. Drackman threw his body over the wounded man and when the artillery round went off, flying shrapnel shattered the Lieutenant's leg and that small piece of shrapnel found its way into and through his arm pit. The tragedy is that the man he thought was wounded was already dead. He had tried to protect a man who was already dead from his wounds. Later, while he was at the 121st Evacuation Hospital in Seoul, Lt. Drackman was awarded the Silver Star for heroism by the Commanding General of the 45th Infantry Division. It was time to evacuate Lt.

Drackman to the 121st Evacuation Hospital in Seoul. A helicopter was called and soon arrived. Father Benson requested that he be allowed to accompany the Lieutenant. His request was granted. He remained with the Lieutenant for several days; he stayed with him until he was completely out of danger. Something had transpired between Lieutenant Drackman and Father Benson. The relationship went far deeper than was ordinarily the case between the chaplain and a casualty. I believe I am correct in saying that a bond of brotherly love had been forged between the two men, and if both are still living, it wouldn't surprise me one bit if, after all these years, they are still keeping in touch. Unfortunately, the Lieutenant lost his badly damaged leg. Tragic to be sure but, his life was saved. Father Benson would call us daily to give us a report on the Lieutenant's condition. We waited anxiously for that daily report. For all of us who were on duty in the E.R. that morning, the feeling was more like the Lieutenant was a brother rather than just another casualty from one of the 45ths artillery units. And that too, was part of the miracle. The whole episode was a miracle. Even now, I feel so privileged to have been a part of that experience.

A Helicopter Evacuation

Forty-seven years ago I wrote to Bonnie that I witnessed a miracle. I told her that beyond any doubt the Spirit of God was in the E.R. that morning and remained until the Lieutenant was out of danger. For once, the E.R. was quiet. No joking around, no vulgarity, no foul language, only very brief conversations about the Lieutenant and his condition in hushed tones. Oh yes, we had a skilled surgeon that a.m., thank God for that. Dr. Shearer performed wonderfully. There were great medics in the E.R. who, once having been told what to do by Dr. Shearer, went about their work without hesitation. And then, there was father Benson in his Quonset, praying without ceasing until the Lieutenant's life was out of danger and his vital signs restored. Such teamwork I cannot recall ever having seen before or after.

Do I believe in battlefield miracles? Forty-seven years later I can say without equivocation, "you bet I do! I witnessed one."

A Very Ugly American

General Ginder's efforts to root out and transfer the prostitutes back to Seoul was almost fanatic. In the spring of 1953 we had as a company commander, a medical doctor, a Major, whose hobby was horticulture. As such, when time permitted, he would scour the countryside looking for unfamiliar plants, and as he would do so, he would keep his eyes open for any sign of a camp that might suggest a place of location for prostitutes. The prostitutes were wise; they knew that there was a frantic effort to find them and remove them from the area and so they moved often. Just when the M.Ps. thought they had them, they would move on to a new location.

One spring day, however, the Major lucked out. He found the camp of a group of prostitutes quite by accident and without disturbing them, returned to the compound and called the Provost Marshall's office (P.M.) at Division Headquarters. I should point out that the Major just didn't happen to stumble on the prostitute's camp; he located it from a distance using his binoculars. For if he had, they would have fled long before the men from the Provost's Office arrived.

It wasn't too long after his call that a couple of Jeeps with armed M.Ps. and a loud mouthed Captain arrived. The M.Ps. were carrying rifles as well as pistols. Why all the armament? I don't know since I never heard of M.Ps. being attacked by prostitutes. At the same time and in all fairness, they weren't going to a Sunday school picnic either. The M.Ps. and the Captain with the Major in the lead soon disappeared over a hill. I don't recall how long they were gone, but it was the loud mouth of the Captain from the P.Ms. office that alerted me to the fact that they were back in the compound. I stepped out of the E.R., and it was a sorry but also a humorous spectacle that met my eyes. Here they came: our company commander, the officer from the P.Ms. office, three M.Ps., four very young girls and an older Mama Sahn, who obviously was in charge of the girls.

Many G.Is. as well as indigenous Korean personnel had heard the ruckus and were standing around as the parade approached the E.R. They were coming to the E.R. so the doctors could examine the girls for V.D., gonorrhea most likely. Suddenly, the officer from the P.Ms. office shouted out in a voice loud enough to be heard throughout the compound; "Major, Major, the General said that if we caught the sons of bitches, we should shoot them." Now I might have understood the frustration of the Captain but, that outburst was entirely uncalled for. Those "sons of bitches" were girls that I would guess were between the ages of 15 and 18. A couple of Korean men were standing close to me and most, if not all, Korean indigenous personnel at 120th Clearing Company could both speak and understand English. I could see the hatred written on their faces. The girls may have been prostitutes but, at the same time they were their girls, and they could do nothing about the vulgar language or the girl's situation. The Captain, of course, did not get his way since the Major would not hear of harming the girls. However, even today, I wonder if the Major had concurred with his suggestion to shoot the girls, if the Captain would not have done so. After all, he had the Commanding General's permission. V.D. was epidemic in the Division and this fact was giving it a very bad name. And at that moment, he appeared angry enough to commit homicide. At this time, Korean officials had absolutely no authority over American military personnel. He could have shot them or had them shot with impunity.

As the girls approached where I was standing, I had a chance to take a good look at them. First, they were very young, second they were very frightened. Most likely they couldn't understand what the Captain had said, but they could understand his wrath, and third, they were filthy both in body and clothing. Their faces were dirty, their hands were dirty, and they exuded a foul odor. All four of the girls were wearing trousers made from a G.I. wool blanket, and the trousers were stained from their crotch halfway to their knees. Small wonder that those who had intercourse with them contracted gonorrhea, for after all, gonorrhea is a disease of filth. Water was scarce in Korea. One could walk in the hills and seldom find a pool or a flowing stream of water. They had neither water with which to wash or the time to do so since they had to keep on the move. The Mama Sahn was dressed in a black jacket and black trousers. All five were brought into the E.R. The girls were examined by the doctors, which must have been a nauseating procedure. All were found to have gonorrhea and all were given penicillin. After the exams, the girls and the Mama Sahn piled into the jeeps and drove out of the compound.

The Korean men had gathered into small groups and were talking and gesturing wildly among themselves. I think I can say without fear of contradiction that we didn't make any friends among those Korean men on that spring day and all because of one loud mouthed ugly American.

There is an interesting sequel to this event. When the women were removed from their camp and, I assume, were given a one way trip to Seoul; the M.Ps. came back to destroy the camp. What they found surprised even them. The place was full of military equipment: G.I. cots, G.I. blankets, G.I. under clothing, etc., etc., and even a metal bed complete with spring, for the Mama Sahn most likely. A bit of investigating revealed that one of the sergeants working in the supply tent supplied the girls with the G.I. equipment. In return he had access to four girls and all the sex he could handle. On the other hand, that metal bed, complete with springs, might have been his and used by him when he had sex with the girls. Needless to say, the M.Ps. came and got him. I never did hear what happened to him, but I imagine he was busted in rank and, because he had bartered with government equipment, was most likely given a suite in the division stockade.

ROBERT'S ORDEAL

Basic Training was to be a time of learning, learning to take orders and not question them, learning not to question superiors, learning to survive in combat. It was a time of discipline and a time for the Army to show just how stupid it could be.

Example No. 1 Physical Education was a twice a day activity, morning and evening. So far as getting one into shape, it was a worthwhile routine. However, with P.E., the Army was given a chance to reveal its stupidity. One of the men in my company had an emergency appendectomy. Now no one was going to be in the base hospital any longer than absolutely necessary. The hospitalized individual may not be fully recovered but so long as he could walk and take care of his own needs, feed himself, clean up around his area in the barracks, etc., he was usually released. And so it was with the fellow who had the appendectomy. Now one would think that common sense would dictate that a person who had just undergone an appendectomy a few days earlier would be excused from P.E. until full healing had taken place. Not so. The very first day he was back from the hospital, he had to fall out for calisthenics. As we went through the various exercises, he was having considerable difficulty bending, touching his toes, twisting his torso, etc., which the cadre member leading the calisthenics noticed. He got on the fellow, dressing him down, warning him that he was to do the exercises as he was supposed to. He couldn't; he experienced too much pain. This really angered the cadre leader, so he stopped the exercises, came down off his platform, walked over to the fellow, dressed him down again for goofing off and then told him to get down on his stomach, lock his hands behind his back and belly crawl. So down he went, trying his best to do what the calisthenics leader ordered him to do.

In a very short time, he could go no farther and very soon he was convulsing on the ground. Too late, the cadre member realized something was seriously wrong with him. He had one of the men run to the C.P. to have an ambulance sent. When the poor fellow arrived at the hospital, the medics discovered that all of the stitches had pulled loose from his appendectomy incision. Of course, he had to be hospitalized again. The cadre member leading calisthenics was a wise guy as well as a tough guy, so most of us in the Company waited to hear that he had gotten his butt in a sling and would be replaced for making the fellow do calisthenics so shortly after his operation. He didn't. Most likely he wasn't even reprimanded, for the very next morning, bright and early, he was up on his stand, leading calisthenics and being just as mean as ever. I can't recall if I ever saw the fellow with the appendectomy back in the company. Because of time lost, once he was released, he may well have been transferred to another company not as far along in basic training.

Example No. 2 On another occasion, the company had just come off a three-day bivouac, a field exercise. This was in December or January of 1952/1953 and the exercise had been accompanied by rain, snow and mud, always mud. We got back to the company area around 3:00 p.m. with our field equipment filthy, dirty and packed with mud. Field exercise or no field exercise, we would be standing inspection at 9:00 a.m. the following morning. Now in order to get ready for the Saturday morning inspection, all field gear had to be cleaned and the barracks floor scrubbed. Personal matters, such as a haircut, pressed uniform, polished boots, etc. also had to be attended to. And yes, once I got settled at Camp Pickett, I had my hair cutting tools sent and instead of scrubbing floors, I cut hair. Needless to say, there was very little sleep that night. This, however, was not new so we immediately went to work, and by 9:00 a.m. Saturday, we were ready to stand inspection. As the officers came into the barracks going from soldier to soldier, checking dress, field pack, and his area; they came to Robert's area. Everything was going okay until one of the inspectors pulled Robert's entrenching tool off the shelf behind his bed. Robert had forgotten to clean his entrenching tool, which was covered with mud, and even worse, rust. Of course, he received a demerit and the entire company was restricted to the base for the remainder of the weekend. Being restricted happened quite often so it was nothing new.

The First Sergeant, however, was furious with Robert. He made him go out to the Company parade area, shoulder his dirty entrenching tool like he would a rifle, and for two hours march around the area shouting at the top of his lungs, "I'm a stupid S.O.B., I'm a stupid S.O.B." Now the barracks all faced the parade ground and there were 250 men in the company. Each time someone would go into or leave the barracks, he couldn't help but see and hear Robert. In addition, anyone passing through the area would also see this spectacle. It had to be so humiliating to Robert that I am sure more than one tear was shed. And all and only because he forgot to clean his entrenching tool, which in the frenzy to get ready for inspection, would have been easy to do. And pray tell, what was gained by making Robert suffer like that? Robert was a stupid S.O.B.? Hardly. It was the First Sergeant who was the stupid S.O.B.

Once the 45th Division arrived in Korea and went up on line, a "patrol type" war was instituted, a patrol war that sought out contact with the enemy. In commenting on this type of war, the Commanding General of the 45th Division said the following: "This patrolling is the finest training I have seen. We would not know where the enemy is without them. It can be compared to life insurance: I want the men to know we are doing it for their protection." Good and well if you weren't on one of the patrols; not so good if you were. As one G.I. put it: "We had to learn the ways of a patrol type of war. In order for a patrol to be credited with making enemy contact you had to exchange small arms fire. It wasn't sufficient to get close enough to his position to see him and direct mortar and artillery fire on him, it had to be small arms." From, THUNDERBIRD: A History of the 45th Infantry Division, pp 12 & 13-No publication date). Since contact with the enemy was essential for the patrol to be a success and since there had to be an exchange of small arms fire, most likely, someone was going to get hurt. During the night time hours, both American and Chinese or North Koreans sent out patrols. Much of the fighting in Korea took place during the nighttime hours.

One early morning an ambulance pulled into the compound and up to the E.R. I was working nights so I went out with another medic to see what was in the ambulance. When I opened the door, a number of walking wounded stepped out. One man was on a stretcher. I went inside the ambulance and grabbed the litter where the man's head rested. When I stepped outside, imagine my surprise when I found myself looking into the face of Robert. I didn't even know he was in the 45th Division. I noticed he was in an extreme state of agitation and had a look of terror in his eyes. Another thing I noticed was the very foul smell of a body that hadn't been washed in a long time. When we got him into the E.R., we discovered that he had injured his back and could not walk. He would have to be evacuated, but first he needed to be cleaned up. We literally cut his clothing from his body since it was filthy and caked with mud and grime. Of course, he recognized me as I recognized him and after we got him cleaned up I sat beside his stretcher and we talked. I asked Robert what had happened to him. That night Robert accompanied a contact patrol as its medic. Some distance out from the trench or bunker, they were ambushed by an enemy patrol and a brief firefight followed. According to the good General, that was a successful patrol. A couple of men fled and several were wounded. I can't recall if any men were killed in the ambush.

In an effort to escape, Robert fell backward off a small embankment injuring his back. He was unable to move. The American troops that were able to escape the area did. However, a number of the wounded, including Robert, lay in the grass where they had fallen. The enemy then commenced seeking out the wounded men, and when they found them, they would fire a killing bullet into their heads. Robert said they got so close to him that he could hear their footsteps and see the grass move from their shuffling feet. He was certain he would be discovered and would be killed.

The enemy soldiers went back and forth wanting to make sure that none of the wounded survived. All this time, in pain and not able to move his lower body, Robert remained absolutely quiet. Obviously, he was not found. Later more men were sent out to bring in the dead and wounded. Of the wounded, Robert was the only one to survive. Small wonder he had such a wild look in his eyes. I recall him saying, "Dick, I thought at any moment they were going to find me and, like the others, I would be killed. We evacuated Robert, and I never saw him again.

I couldn't help recall that Saturday a.m. back at Camp Pickett, Virginia, when in the rush to be ready for Saturday's inspection, Robert's dirty entrenching tool was found and he was subjected to such total humiliation. What the First Sergeant did to Robert was totally uncalled for and, so far as I was concerned, revealed once again, just how stupid the Army could be. Come to think of it, the sergeant that subjected Robert to such humiliation was the same sergeant that tore into me for speaking without permission to do so.

DOCTORS DO BURY THEIR MISTAKES: SOMETIMES

I must say that Clearing Company, 120th Medical Battalion, was blessed with good doctors. Most of our doctors were draftees, not career men, and, as such, were doctors first and officers second. From time to time we would receive men just out of medical school, and their knowledge about battle casualties was nil. However, these neophytes learned to deal with them in a very short time; there was no time to learn gradually. When casualties arrived in the E.R., the doctors would grab a wounded man and go to work. Soon, all were experts, whether they had practiced extensively in the U.S. or were just out of medical school.

One of the things that stumped them, however, were diseases common to Koreans but new to American and other Western U.N.(United Nations) personnel. Most notably was H.F. (hemorrhagic fever). Initially, G.Is. who contracted the disease received no treatment because the doctors didn't know how to treat H.F. Many men died before a treatment was devised. Hemorrhagic fever is a disease that eventually causes the kidneys to shut down and, from what I understood, it was a painful and difficult death. Koreans also got hemorrhagic fever. Whereas they would get pretty darn sick, I can't recall any dying from the disease. Over the centuries their bodies had built up immunity to the disease. G.Is. had no immunity whatsoever. Aside from H.F., the doctors encountered diseases not frequently seen in their stateside practice but, none the less, covered in medical school. Thus they at least had a textbook familiarity with them.

Intestinal parasites were epidemic among Koreans. It got so that every time a Korean soldier or indigenous person showed up with abdominal cramps or pain, without so much as an examination, the doctors would begin the usual treatment for intestinal parasites. Within a couple of days, victims would be on their feet and ready to return to their respective outfits. Of course, this was primarily a consequence of using human feces as a fertilizer and the unsanitary practices of the Koreans. It would be a rare occurrence when hands were washed before eating. We were told to avoid eating Korean food at all costs. The one time I did get to Seoul, a street vendor had a table of the most delicious looking apples. As much as I would have liked one, I passed them by, not because the inside of the apple was contaminated with parasites, it was the outside I had to worry about. Since the Koreans did not wash their hands frequently, it was their handling of the apples that contaminated them.

In spite of treating every kind of wound and disease imaginable, doctors did make mistakes. I worked with Dr. Kretzchmar and am reminded of two fellows that were his charges: one died from a disease that was misdiagnosed, and the other, a battle casualty, survived only because of good fortune and not because of the way Dr. Kretzchmar treated his wound.

One morning an ambulance arrived from one of the regimental aid stations. When the patient was brought in to the E.R. sitting upright on the stretcher, I thought this rather odd. Dr. Kretzchmar happened to be on duty. He questioned the medic from Regimental Aid Station who told him that at 8:00 p.m. the previous evening the fellow came to see him complaining of a rather severe headache. The medic gave him a couple of aspirin, and the fellow returned to his tent. By morning, not only had the painful headache increased in intensity many fold; now he also had a severe backache that was gradually getting worse. His back caused him great pain especially when he lay down. The G.I. wasn't wearing a shirt, and I noticed that the skin over his entire chest and back was covered with huge blotches. Now sometimes hemorrhagic fever, in its early stages, will manifest itself with blotchy patches on the skin, although it was more common for the skin to be covered with small petechia. Dr. Kretzchmar felt quite sure he had a patient in the early stages of hemorrhagic fever. He wanted to examine the G.I. but, found it difficult to do so with him sitting up. I recall the doctor telling the fellow, "Come on now, it can't be that painful for you to lie down," and with that he pushed the man back by placing his hands on his shoulders. Immediately the man cried out in pain. By this time Dr. Kretzchmar was getting impatient with the G.I. and, suspecting H.F., called a helicopter to transport him to the 121st Evacuation Hospital. If I remember correctly, he rode inside the chopper thus enabling him to sit up. Most evacuees were placed in a litter and strapped to the landing bar of the chopper. It was viewed as a routine evacuation and soon the fellow was forgotten.

At about 5:00 p.m. the phone rang. The call was from the 121st Evacuation Hospital, and the doctor at the other end of the line wanted to talk to Dr. Kretzchmar. I noticed that Kretzchmar was quiet, doing a lot more listening than talking. Finally he hung up the phone and just stood by the desk in silence. He turned to me and said, "Waltner, I goofed, I really goofed. Remember the fellow I evacuated this a.m. with a diagnosis of H.F.? Well, he died this afternoon at 4:00. He didn't have H.F., he had meningococcal meningitis, and to think, I thought he was gold bricking when he complained about a back that was excruciatingly painful. And here I tried to force him to lie down. Why didn't I suspect meningitis? The painful back should have alerted me to the fact he didn't have H.F." With that he left the E.R. On several occasions, however, he brought up the fact that he had tried to force the man to lie down and thought he was gold bricking when he said he couldn't and cried out in pain. At the time I thought Kretzchmar was unnecessarily brusque and hard on the man. The incident really bothered him and rightfully so. It also haunted me since it was obvious the man was in extreme pain. Meningococcal meningitis is extremely contagious and a number of us had come into close contact with the man. We were all at risk of developing this often fatal disease. So at 2:00 a.m. the next morning, the entire company fell out in formation and all of us, not just those who had come in contact with the man, but all of us were given heavy doses of sulfa drugs which we continued to take for a couple of days. Why 2:00 a.m.? So everyone would be present to take their measure of sulfa. Men on duty were given sulfa at their workstation. Fortunately, so far as I know, no one else came down with the disease, not at Clearing Company and not in the regiment.

It was a sobering experience and one that reminded me of just how fragile life really is. At 8:30 one evening this G.I. went to see his medic to get something for a headache. Early the next morning, not only did he have a splitting headache, his back pained him so badly that he could not lie down. By 4:00 p.m. on the same day, he was dead. From first symptoms, a headache, to death all in less than 24 hours.

On another occasion, when we were having a run of casualties, a fellow came in on a stretcher with a bullet wound to the abdomen. There was no bleeding. The man was conscious, smoking a cigarette, quite talkative and, apparently in no pain. Most likely he had been given morphine. Dr. Kretzchmar was his doctor. His intestine was bulging through the bullet hole but really not all that bad. Dr. Kretzchmar took several 4X4 gauze bandages, placed them over the wound, forcing the intestine back into the abdominal cavity and then taped them to his abdomen. He ordered an ambulance evacuation to an ASH down the road to the south. The fellow was loaded aboard the ambulance and it was on its way. Dr. Kretzchmar moved to the next casualty and soon the man with the bullet wound to the abdomen was but a dim memory.

It must have been about two hours later when the phone rang. I answered and a very irate voice on the other end asked to speak to Dr. Kretzchmar. I called him over to the phone. Again, it was a one-way conversation. I could tell from the look on his face that some thing pretty heavy was coming over that phone. When he finally put it down, he turned to me and said, "Waltner, I goofed again. Then he proceeded to tell me that the call was from the ASH unit. The doctor on the other end asked Kretzchmar, "What in the hell kind of a doctor are you? Don't you know enough to check for an entry wound? Had you simply turned the man over, you would have discovered that the bullet did not enter the abdomen; it entered his back and exited his abdomen. You should have never sent that man to us in an ambulance. Bouncing over those rough roads as the ambulance did, you can be darn lucky he didn't start bleeding, for if he had, he most likely would have bled to death before reaching us." Once again, Dr. Kretzchmar had very little to say. He just stared off into space for a spell before going back to work.

I thought to myself, Now why didn't I think of turning him over? I had hunted plenty back in South Dakota before being drafted, and I knew a bullet with a full metal jacket and fired from a high powered rifle can penetrate a lot of mass. I should have known that there was an entry wound somewhere. Most likely, had the bullet entered the man's stomach it would not have made a hole large enough for his intestine to protrude. On the other hand, because the skin of the abdomen is stretched rather tightly, it is possible that it could have made a hole that large. So I guess both Dr. Kretzchmar and I goofed, but it was he who caught hell. It was he who should have known "that you always check for another wound when the wound is made by a bullet." This time Kretzchmar was lucky, the man didn't bleed and made a good recovery.

WHEN EAST MEETS WEST

When the trappings of a modern, scientifically oriented and technologically proficient culture and society come into contact with a society and culture steeped in traditionalism, there is bound to be conflict of one kind or another. I have already alluded to some of this conflict.

When I arrived in Korea, the Korean Army was made up primarily of young men, very young men. What standing army South Korea had at the time of the invasion, was pretty well wiped out when the North invaded the South. In order to rebuild its army, the South undertook an extensive program of drafting men. Since South Korea was a traditional society, it is not stretching it to say a majority of the young men came from rural areas. I say young men; actually many were not even that. They were boys. I would imagine that boys drafted from cities such as Seoul and Pusan showed some sophistication and some knowledge of American culture and matching technology. However, boys from the rural areas would find both very foreign.

It is to be remembered that following World War II the United States kept a military presence in South Korea, which was supposed to have been training a South Korean Army fully capable of repelling an invasion from the North should one occur. Obviously, the U.S. forces were not doing their job since the North Koreans swept south with only limited resistance.

Quite suddenly these boys found themselves in an army equipped with the latest technology in weapons and machines utilized by the seven American divisions in Korea. At least I believe it was seven. I have absolutely no idea what the laws pertaining to firearms ownership were in Korea back in the early 50s. I would guess that they were very restrictive, and most of these boys knew little or nothing about modern weaponry. It was, therefore, not uncommon to see Korean boys who were the victims of accidental, self inflicted gun shot wounds. Whenever a group of these men, boys, would come into the 120th Clearing Company compound, I kept my eyes trained on where the barrels of the rifles and carbines were pointed.

If it were not for the insignia on their uniforms and the physical appearance of the men, I would not have known the South Korean Army was the South Korean Army. The uniforms were American, the weapons were American, the tents were American and the vehicles were American. What wasn't American was the discipline. Several times upon making a move, we settled in a place that had formerly been occupied by a Korean military outfit. They were always a disaster. Junked armament and refuse were scattered everywhere. Just cleaning up such an area was a major undertaking. And yet, I was told that when disobeying orders, the officers would often physically assault the recruits. Whether or not this was true, I cannot say. However, given the attitude of the officers when they came to pick up a soldier recuperating at Clearing Company or given the harsh response to our request for the Korean doctors to treat as quickly as possible the woman with the third degree burns to her legs, I would not doubt the accuracy of the report.

The training of the young men also left much to be desired. One of the constant concerns the American Army had was that when the ROK (Republic of Korea) Divisions were on line and came under heavy enemy pressure that they would "bug out." That is leave their positions and retreat to a rear area. When that happened an American Division in reserve would have to be rushed to the front to fill the gap. Being aware of this, when the Chinese did attack a Korean Division, they would attack it with much ferocity.

Some of the incidents of unfamiliarity with modern technology had a humorous twist to them. Many more were tragic. The power we had at Clearing Company came from a generator run by a Jeep motor. At best, the outflow of electricity was erratic. I had acquired a much used and abused radio, however, it could still pick up a few stations. It was just before Christmas and the Army stations were playing Christmas music. In order to avoid burning it up with a power surge, I purchased a voltage regulator from the P.X. and connected it to the radio. With it, the power coming into the radio could be regulated. I knew the three Katusa boys living with us in the squad tent had no idea what a voltage regulator was. I had told them it was okay for them to listen to the radio but not to touch the regulator. They could not grasp how that box with the knob could control the amount of current flowing into the radio. One evening I was working late when one of my fellow tent mates came to see me. He informed me that one of the Korean boys had started fooling with the voltage regulator and cranked the control knob to a very high level of voltage input. Immediately the radio burned out. He said it started smoking as if it were on fire. Initially I was angry and the Korean was going to get a good chewing out. My tent mate told me that the fellow had said, "The sergeant is going to kill me." By the time I got to the tent I had cooled off. I walked inside and the poor fellow looked as if he expected to receive a beating. I asked him what he had done. He pointed to the voltage regulator and indicated that he had turned the knob. Now the Katusa boys could understand a little English, not much, but a little. He was sitting at the table next to the smoking radio. I sat down beside him and said, "Now do you see why the Sergeant told you not to touch the box?" In the best way he could, he said he was sorry. At that point I felt sorry for him, picked up the radio on my way out of the tent and tossed it into a trash barrel as I went back to work in the E.R. Needless to say, we missed the radio, we missed the Christmas music, and it would be some time before we got another.

One April morning in 1953, two Korean soldiers, boys they were, were brought to Clearing Company in the back of a Korean (really American) ambulance. Someone found a flamethrower where it shouldn't have been, picked it up, started fooling around with it and it ignited. The flame leaped out of the muzzle and caught the two young men squarely in the face. By the time they got to Clearing Company, their faces and heads were swollen to nearly twice the normal size. Their eyes were closed, either from damage or the swelling, their hair was burned off, and fluids were seeping from their faces. I helped carry one from the ambulance, holding his head up off the stretcher. When I released his head, the scalp from the back of his head came off in my hands. We did what we could, medically speaking, and quickly had them evacuated. Just before leaving, one of the boys, speaking through badly swollen lips, begged our interpreter to take a gun and kill him. I doubt they survived but, if they did, their faces must have been horribly disfigured.

On another occasion shortly after the incident with the flamethrower, several truckloads of Korean soldiers were being transported to the front line. Now most roads in Korea, especially those near the battle lines, were dozed out in a hurry and were rough and narrow and always dangerous. One truck passed another and since the road was too narrow for two trucks to be side by side simultaneously, which any experienced driver would have known, the truck on the outside was forced off the road. It rolled down a 30-foot embankment. One soldier was killed instantly while the others received all kinds of injuries. Fifteen of the injured soldiers were brought into the E.R. at one time. There were broken arms, broken legs, back injuries, internal injuries, facial injuries and fractured skulls. I was taking the blood pressure of one of the injured men, whose systolic pressure was 80 and there was no discernable diastolic pressure. It looked like we were losing him. We quickly started an IV of dextrin solution, and in a short time his blood pressure bounced up to 110/80, which is normal. Poor fellows, all were mere boys and fresh recruits. After our life saving procedures, all were transferred to a Korean hospital.

And there were other similar accidents. On February 9th a truckload of ROK soldiers was brought to the E.R. Like the truck above, the truck had gone off the side of a road and rolled with the same consequences to the soldiers. They experienced every kind of fracture imaginable. On the very next day another truck rolled off the road and these men too were brought to Clearing Company. During the course of 15 months in Korea, I saw many Korean soldiers and Korean civilians injured as the result of vehicle accidents.

So many of these accidents reflected an unfamiliarity with American technology and they indicate the kinds of tragedies that occurred when the machine age was suddenly thrust upon men who, if they had weapons, were most likely muzzle loaders and for whom the fastest means of transportation was an oxen drawn cart.

THE MANY FACES OF KOREA

"The countryside is magnificent, high towering peaks covered with green foliage. Some appear so high that they are hidden in the clouds. Really, Darling, it is a beautiful country and I can certainly see why Korea is called, 'Land of the Morning Calm'." And on December 14th, 1953: "You should see the big moon tonight, it really is beautiful. The skies are clear with only an occasional white cloud scudding across the face of the moon. It isn't very cold either, a perfect night for romance, however, the romancing will have to be left to the Koreans."

I must admit that in spite of all the griping and senseless decisions made by the Army brass, the Orient was getting into my blood. I found it enchantingly beautiful. One night while I was serving as Sergeant of the Guard and walking to the guard tent, the moon was just coming over the Eastern Mountains. The valleys were full of a very fine mist, and when the moonlight hit the mist, the world seemed to light up in a bluish, violet light. It was breathtakingly beautiful. One cannot imagine how beautiful unless witnessed personally. I had never seen such beauty as I saw in Korea and Japan. In Japan I saw some of the most spectacular sunsets. And this is coming from a former flat lander where beautiful sunsets are a rather common occurrence. This fantastic moonlight wasn't the only such experience; in fact, when the moon was full and the humidity high, such beauty was not uncommon. Neither was it uncommon to watch the fog roll in from the ocean, filling first the valleys and then rising to completely engulf the low lying mountains. Clearing Company, 120th Medical Battalion, at this time, was located high up off the valley floor, giving those who were interested a commanding view of the scenes just described. It was at times like these that I did not mind guard duty.

"February is producing snow, lots of snow, heavy rains followed by snow and bitter, bitter cold but, it also presented me with a most beautiful moonlit night. It seems just when I was about to give up on the weather, the skies cleared and out came that beautiful full moon. The ground is covered with a fresh blanket of snow; it hasn't yet been disturbed. I stepped out of the tent and looked across the valley to the snow capped mountains and fog shrouded valleys and the sight was beautiful, beautiful enough to make me forget, at least for the moment, all the misery of the rain and cold. I know I will never forget the beauty of Korea under a full moon."

Of course, Korea had another face; it had many faces. There were three enemies to watch for in Korea. One enemy carried weapons, another enemy was disease and the third enemy was the extremely cold winter. The 38th Parallel really isn't that far from Manchuria, known for its ferocious winters. Once winter set in, it was not possible to keep warm, really warm. The only thing keeping us from the elements was a piece of canvas stretched over a wooden frame. And, the Korean winter seemed interminably long. There were two pot-bellied stoves in each tent, but we were never allowed to turn them high enough to heat the tent.

In the fall of 1953, more of the idiocy of the military was revealed. Someone got the crazy idea to have a contest, a contest which amounted to seeing which outfit could wait the longest before allowing the troops to light the stoves for what little heat they generated. Though I never found out, I have a hunch the officers were not involved in this contest, and they enjoyed the benefit of heat in their tents.

The days were cold and the nights were down right frigid. It is to be remembered that we were in the mountains, and the elevation played no small part in the temperatures, especially night time temperatures. We started to see an increasing number of men on sick call suffering from upper respiratory illnesses but even this could not budge the brass to give the order to turn on the heat.

The 30th of October rolled around and we still had not received permission to light the stoves. Other than the hospital wards, there was no place to go to warm up. Then just one day later, November 1, the order finally came down from Division Headquarters to light the stoves. I never did find out who cried "uncle" first. To give the reader an idea of what the winters in Korea were like, I compare them to the winters in South Dakota, winters that I was most familiar with. Temperatures often dropped to well below zero and there was snow, not a lot of snow, but snow nonetheless. At times the wind blew near blizzard strength. When that happened, those little pot-bellied stoves did nothing to make the tents warm. One learned to live with misery. Oh yes, we had cold weather clothing, but it did very little to keep one warm. It was common to get up in the morning and to have to break the ice in our helmets. Why the helmets? They were used as our wash basins. And since the stove put out little heat, having warm water with which to shave or wash was a very infrequent happening. There were, of course, breaks in the cold and then for a brief time comfort was experienced. After only a few days of this we would be plunged again into the deep-freeze. Many men suffered cold weather injury. For some reason known only to the military, it steadfastly denied this for 47 years. It was only in 1997 that it was finally acknowledged that many, many men had suffered cold weather injury. The cold was bad enough, however, since Korea was a peninsula only 100 miles wide, the high humidity only made the cold seem colder. Needless to say, the winter of 1953/54 was a tough one as I am sure were most Korean winters.

One yearned for spring and the return of warm temperatures and when those warm temperatures arrived, they were a Godsend. Oh sure, the summers were hot. In 1953 we had a few days when the thermometer reached 115 degrees and as with the cold of winter, the high humidity made it feel a lot hotter. The heat of summer, for me at least, paled in comparison to the cold of winter. As mentioned, being raised in south eastern South Dakota, a land known for its extreme cold and frequent blizzards, I handled the winters very well before Korea. After Korea, however, I discovered that my toleration level for cold weather was very low. I was one of the men who experienced cold weather injury and still suffer from Raynaud's phenomenon brought on by the injury. As I was warned at the time the diagnosis was made, this condition has only worsened as I have gotten older. The winter cold of Korea was indeed a formidable enemy.

In the spring of the year, the countryside took on a beauty all its own. Like most, if not all of the Orient, rice is the main agricultural crop. To the rear of the military installations, it seemed that all of the land was divided into small parcels and planted in rice. It was not my good fortune to go often to these areas that lay behind the military installations. In fact, only once in 15 months did I have an opportunity to go south to Seoul. It was in spring and as we left the last military installation, field upon field upon field of rice paddies greeted the eye. This was in mid to late May. The paddies were flooded and everyone who could was planting rice. This tedious task was done by hand. The rice shoots had to be pressed deep into the flooded soil. Elderly men, elderly women, young men, young women and teenagers were all in the field planting rice. Even mothers with infants were not excused. The baby was simply carried in a sling like affair on the mother's back, a very ingenious device and idea. When it came time to feed the baby, the mother would cease planting for a moment, swing the baby to the front of her body so it could gain access to her breast, and then return to planting rice. At that time, as the rice was being planted and many fields remained unplanted, the appearance of the countryside was like any agricultural area just coming alive after a long winter: a uniform brown broken by ponds of muddy water. However, in mid-June when I left for Inchon and the boat ride home, the countryside was beautiful. As far as the eye could see stretched a patchwork quilt of many hues of green. What wasn't good, however, was the odor. As mentioned previously, Koreans fertilized their rice fields with human feces. Now it got hot in Korea, as hot in summer as cold in winter. And along with the heat came an almost unbelievable stench. It was so bad that it seemed as if it invaded every pore of the body. I imagine the Koreans got used to it. I wonder if any G.Is. did? I didn't get into the agricultural area often enough to find out if I could adjust to it. If indeed our reaction to odors is culturally induced as some claim, then I would assume in time anyone who lived in Korea long enough would get used to the odor. But for my very much American nose, it was almost more than I could bear.

The Koreans were very hard working people who suffered plenty. The invasion of the South by the North was devastating. More than likely, few families escaped the effect of the invasion. Ground that had previously been planted in rice became battlefields. The people were driven from the land and it wasn't until after the cease-fire that they moved back onto at least some of the fields that previously had been under cultivation. And, of course, those fields were mined, always presenting a danger to the farmers brave enough to attempt to put them back into production.

One effect of the war was that many beasts of burden, primarily oxen, were killed. The rice paddies, before they were flooded and planted, had to be ploughed. Without a team of oxen this could be a formidable task. One day, I saw three farmers ploughing a rice field. Two men were pulling what appeared to be a very primitive one-bottom plough while the third steered it. That task had to be back breaking. But still, I never heard them complain. It seemed to me they never complained although that may well be an overstatement.

One day I had to go to an ASH to check on a patient. My driver and I climbed a rather steep, low mountain and when we reached the top, we were halted by M.Ps. who told us that a military exercise was underway on top of the hill. Now we were high enough and close enough to see the exercise. There in a newly ploughed rice field were two or three tanks that had locked a track and spun around until a fairly deep crater had been dug. Jets would come screaming over the crest of the hill only a few feet off the ground and the gunners in the tanks would rotate their turrets trying to keep their machine guns trained on the jets. This went on for some time. As I looked around, I saw a small group of farmers with tools in hand, standing off to the side watching the exercise with bewilderment written on their faces. Days of hard work destroyed in a few short minutes. After the exercise, the tanks drove off; no attempt was made to repair the damage to the rice field. And, I saw no one complain to the M.Ps. or other officers who were watching and overseeing the exercise. Who could they complain to when the only ones available were the ones who approved the damage to their field?

Koreans who were not military personnel also became casualties of war. And, unfortunately, not all the bullets fired at them came from the enemy to the north. One day a teen-aged boy was brought to the E.R. in a jeep. I was informed that he had been shot by a G.I. I can't recall why. Some men didn't need much of a reason. He was shot with a 30 caliber Ml Carbine. The bullet entered his buttock and exited his penis. He sat on the edge of a stretcher not uttering a word, no tears, no crying although fear was written across his face. If I remember correctly, as the bullet passed through his lower body, the examining doctor did not believe any vital internal organs were hit, however, the damage to his penis was considerable and he would have to be evacuated to a rear area hospital where a urologist would attempt to repair the damage. I asked the doctor on duty if he thought the boy would ever again be able to experience an erection. I recall what the doctor said. He said it depended on how extensive the damage to his corpus cavernosa was and whether or not any damage to the nerves controlling erection occurred as the bullet passed through his lower body. I didn't know much about impotency back then but I thought to myself, how sad it would be if the young man would never be able to have sex with a woman and would never be able to father a child. His stoicism as he looked at his damaged penis was remarkable.

On another occasion, an old Papa Sahn was brought to the E.R. Like the boy just mentioned, he had been shot by a G.I. Again, I do not recall the circumstances. This time the gun used was a 45 automatic pistol. The bullet entered his coccyx. The doctors were fearful that it had continued its path and had tore up his colon. Like the young man, he was evacuated to an ASH. The old man lay on the floor uttering the words, "Etei, etei, I go, I go." Later I asked one of our interpreters what the old man meant by etei, etei, I go, I go. The interpreter said that he was saying that he was going to die. Indeed, we all thought he was going to die. However, in his case as it turned out, the prognosis was most positive. A couple days later I had to go to the ASH to which he was evacuated to check on a patient. It was noon time and the patients were eating lunch. I saw the old man squatting close to the floor, in the typical Korean squat, eating from a tray piled high with food. I asked one of the medics if this wasn't the old Papa Sahn that was sent from Clearing Company with the bullet hole in his tailbone. Yes, it was the same Papa Sahn. I said, "We thought he was so badly wounded that he was close to death." The medic then told me that the bullet had hit the coccyx had penetrated only an inch or two and had really caused no damage other than to the tailbone. Papa Sahn would be fine and would be dismissed in a few days. I was one happy G.I.

The reader might be wondering why were the two G.Is. who had shot the boy and the Papa Sahn not arrested and either court marshaled or imprisoned for attempted murder? First, the military paid scant attention to such incidents. The G.I. could have said, "I caught him stealing from one of the tents." In the case of the boy, the driver of the jeep said the G.I. simply got mad at him. Second, as mentioned earlier the Korean civil authorities had absolutely no jurisdiction over American military personnel. Sadly, these incidents happened and few gave much thought to them. Earlier, I mentioned that whereas some men could not kill, others became very efficient killers and even after the ceasefire, some went on killing. But my point is the absence of complaint, the stoicism exhibited by these two unfortunate individuals.

It wasn't only American G.Is. who became efficient killers. There was a Dutch unit up on line next to the 45th Division regiments. These men were, of course, all volunteers. They were, in effect, soldiers of fortune. One day a Dutch soldier was brought to Clearing Company with severe eye injuries. He had some trash to burn in an incinerator. As he leaned over to throw in his trash, a loaded cartridge already in the incinerator exploded blinding both eyes. He spoke good English so one day I sat down besides his cot and we visited. He told me this was his third tour of duty in Korea. I asked him why he would want to come back three times. His response was kind of a shocker. He came back because he liked to kill; killing for him was a profession. He also told me that one day, they (the Dutch) got word of an impending Chinese attack scheduled for that evening. The Chinese would be coming up what we out here in the west call a box canyon. The Dutch soldiers lined the rim of the canyon as they waited for the Chinese to put in an appearance. They let them get a good ways into the canyon and then ambushed them with devastating consequences for the Chinese. Few escaped. After the shooting was over, some of the Dutch troops went down into the canyon and made a startling discovery. They found approximately one weapon for every three Chinese soldiers. In their human wave attacks, the Chinese were often short of weapons. Their strategy was that as one soldier was killed, another without a weapon would pick up his dead companion's weapon and continue the fight. How does one defeat an enemy that thinks like that? The injured Dutchman thought the ambush and resulting deaths were great sport.

And then, there was the attitude of at least some of the military brass. Organized bandits and thievery were very real problems. One night a gang of bandits broke into the officers' tent, held the men at gunpoint, and robbed them of everything they could get their hands on: cameras, record players, radios, money, guns, etc. It was a very dangerous situation. Fortunately, none of the officers resisted. Immediately after, the General gave orders that any indigenous personnel caught within an Army compound at night should be shot. Guards should shoot to kill. One evening a guard, a fellow I knew well, was walking his two-hour beat. He came around the corner of a tent and ran smack dab into a band of bandits. I can still hear the rat-tat-tat of that M2 Carbine. However, he didn't shoot directly at them, he shot over their heads. When the general heard this, he was furious and was going to have the guard court marshaled for disobeying an order. Fortunately, Captain Lewis, who was the Officer of the Guard, intervened telling the General that his last order to the guards was to shoot over the heads of any indigenous personnel encountered while walking their posts. As displeased as he was, the General changed his mind about the court martial. Still, he issued an order that the guard go to the rifle range for an hour a day for a week, long enough, he felt, for him to learn to shoot. When I spoke to the fellow about this, he laughed. He said he enjoyed shooting the carbine. How else would he have gotten a chance to do some daily target shooting?

SEX AND THE MILITARY

In the spring and summer of 1953, the 45th Infantry Division was plagued with an epidemic of venereal disease. Gonorrhea was the most frequently encountered disease, but venereal warts were beginning to show up. By and large syphilis was not a problem since only occasionally would a case be seen. Some of my Korean friends informed me that until American G.Is. arrived in Korea, syphilis was unknown. That may or may not have been true. At the time, strange as it may seem, it was not known for sure if venereal warts were transmitted sexually. As a consequence, men were being shipped back to the States without being treated for the warts. This had been going on for some time when I read an article in a medical journal, made available by one of the doctors that dealt with venereal warts. The thrust of the article was that a survey of women in the U.S. who had sought medical attention for venereal warts revealed that every one had a husband or boy friend who had been in Korea and had returned with the untreated disease. I have a hunch a lot of marriages ended because of venereal warts, not only because the husband had given it to his wife but also his infidelity was unmasked. I do not recall if treatment was begun while I was in Korea. In fact, since at that time it was rare for doctors to see a case of venereal warts in the U.S., I am not sure doctors knew how to treat it. Standard treatment today may consist of the use of topical ointments. They may also be removed surgically through the use of laser or cyrosurgery. To me they were most unsightly, growing in clusters and looking much like cauliflower. Obviously, the doctor's ignorance on the subject of venereal warts was not a case of ignorance being bliss. Looking back, it seems almost incredible that these men would be sent back to the States to infect wives and girl friends. Since it is something most of the doctors did not see in the States, and since the warts were clustered about the genitals, they had to surmise that the men picked it up somehow and that somehow had to be through sexual intercourse, and that being the case, it was transmissible. All men eligible for rotation to the States were tested for gonorrhea and, if they tested positive, had to remain until a urethral smear proved them negative for the gonorrhea gonococcus. But men with venereal warts went home immediately.

As soon as the weather warmed enough to permit their movement, the prostitutes, largely from Ch'unch'on and Seoul, began to locate close to the various units of the 45th Division as well as other American divisions. When the girls arrived in the hills, they would send a young boy into the compound to tell the men where they could be found. Then the parade started. Of course, the men would sneak out after dark to have their trysts with the girls. One friend told me that the fellows, and not all from Clearing Company to be sure, were lined up waiting their turn to be serviced by the girls. I found the thought of having sex with a girl who just had sex with half a dozen or more other guys and, who most certainly had V.D. to be repugnant. At that time, my understanding of human sexuality was quite limited and although it has increased in the intervening years, I still find it difficult to comprehend how any one could stand in line to have intercourse with a girl who almost certainly had V.D.

The 45th had the unenviable reputation of having the highest V.D. rate of any of the divisions in Korea. This infuriated General P.D. Ginder and he launched into a program to rid the area of prostitutes hoping, thereby, to reduce significantly the rate of V.D. in the Division. Men from the Provost Marshall's office would scour the hills around the military units, and if they found prostitutes, they would be brought to the 120th Clearing Company and examined for V.D. If the exam proved positive, they would be given heavy doses of penicillin and transported back to Seoul. The problem was that in a relatively short time, they would again be back in the hills.

Meanwhile, sick call was besieged with men from all units suffering from gonorrhea. I must admit the General's concerns were well founded. Day after day it was the same. Ambulances rolled into the compound filled with men who had contracted gonorrhea. Some days we would see up to 100 patients; 50 of these would be sent to the lab for gonorrhea smears. Some men were picking it up in Ch'unch'on, however, most were getting it from the girls located in the hills close to our unit. Sergeant Fernandez, Chief Lab Technician, was reaching the breaking point. Now ordinarily, the Sergeant was a compassionate man, but he had reached his limit, especially with men who were back a second or even third time. When obtaining a specimen for a microscopic exam, which was done by inserting a small cotton swab into the penile urethra, he would jam the swab into the urethra causing the patient much pain. Sadistic? I don't think so. Fed up? You bet. I guess he wanted them to know that if they showed up at his lab again, they were going to have a keen memory of having been there.

Meantime the General implemented a number of punishments for men testing positive for V.D. First, they were reduced one grade in rank. For example, a corporal proving positive for V.D. would be busted down to private first class. There seemed to be no decrease in the number of men coming in for urethral smears. Promotions in rank did not come readily; thus, to lose a grade of rank for which one had waited so long was no small punishment. When reduction in rank didn't seem to work, the general next ordered that all men testing positive for V.D., in addition to being reduced in rank, be transferred away from their unit of familiarity to a new and unfamiliar unit. This meant leaving friends behind and having to adjust to a new environment, a pretty harsh punishment. The rate of V.D. may have slowed a little but not much.

The General was naive to assume that by inflicting punishments V.D. within the Division would be eliminated. I have made no mention of officers, only enlisted men. As indicated earlier, officers were a different breed of cats; they may have been from the same genus as the enlisted men, but they constituted a different species. Officers did not get V.D. If this sounds humorous, it is meant to be. One day a Lieutenant came to Clearing Company with a urethral discharge. He was diagnosed with gonorrhea. Since he came through channels, he was handled like any person on sick call. In making up the roster of persons on sick call, he was included, along with his diagnosis, treatment and disposition, he was given penicillin and returned to his outfit. A Daily report of casualties and men on sick call was sent to General Ginder. This report enabled him to keep track of the V.D. cases coming to Clearing Company and also let him know if his preventive steps were having the desired results. The morning following the report, Captain Richmond came into the E.R., walked over to my desk and said; "I got a call from General Ginder and he was furious because the name of the Lieutenant and his diagnosis of gonorrhea appeared on the report. Waltner," he said, with a twinkle in his eyes and a smile on his face that he could not suppress, "there is something you have to know. Officers never get V.D., anything else but not V.D."

Actually, very few officers did come on sick call with V.D. Does this mean they were not sexually active? Of course not. It means they were in a position to be more selective with the girls with whom they were having sex. After all, it was easy for them to slip off to Seoul for a few hours to engage a girl who had regular checks for V.D. Also, whereas enlisted men had to wait seven months for R.&.R. (rest and recuperation) officers went to Japan every three months. Thus, they had some assurance that they were getting fairly regular sex with "clean" girls. In addition, instead of coming in on regular sick call, they could call a doctor, tell him of their condition, come to see the doctor, have a microscopic done and, get the necessary treatment without it ever becoming a part of any record.

It was in the fall and only after the girls had returned to Seoul that the V.D. rate for the Division began to diminish, but only diminish. As unbelievable as it may sound, there were still some girls in the hills in December.

Why so much V.D.? Though I can't put my finger on the precise average age of the enlisted/drafted G.I., it had to be in the very early twenties. Men reach their sexual peak at around eighteen. In fact from pubescence until the peak is reached, the curve reflecting sexual desire and felt sex needs rises quickly and almost vertically. To tell the truth, young men in their late teens and early twenties are a bundle of sexual energy. There is a very good biological reason for this, and biology is usually much more rational than human reasoning. Human females are the most fecund (most likely to conceive) and have trouble free pregnancies during their very late teens and early to mid-twenties. The biology of the sexes is very compatible at this point. A reasonable question is why are these peaks reached at such an early age? I have given much thought to this, and the most logical answer seems to be that homo sapiens is not destined to be long lived. Therefore, if the species is to reproduce itself and raise the young to a point where they can survive without the parents, reproduction must start soon after pubescence is reached. What we tend to forget is that in most traditional societies life expectancy is around 40 years of age. This does not give one much time to reproduce, to contribute his/her genes to the gene pool of the breeding population, and to leave his/her mark on society. Of course, today, with the spread of Western technology, life expectancy is creeping upward almost worldwide if not worldwide. And yet, there are many traditional societies still in existence. In our own American society, life expectancy in 1900 was right around 49 years of age. In 1900, and in many respects, we were still a traditional society. What is a traditional society? It is a society that is pre-scientific, pre-technological and one in which the main economic source is agriculture. We, in American society today enjoy a life expectancy in the 70s, not because our biology has undergone change but because of our scientific and technological advances. We live longer than most traditional people because of the tremendous strides made in medical science and improved nutrition, both dependent on our scientific and technological proficiently. And, of course, one consequence is that women are now beginning to reproduce years later than is the case in traditional societies.

Coddling young people until their early twenties would be unheard of in a traditional society since at twenty they would be middle age. This is a luxury available only in industrial societies.

However, one thing hasn't changed: both men and women are most fecund in their late teens and early twenties. The age of the onset of menopause, which effectively puts an end to the child bearing years, hasn't changed much.

When war comes along and young men are drafted, they enter a sexually segregated society just at the time when they are most desirous of sexual interaction with females. In Korea, the segregation of the sexes was almost complete, especially for men in forward units. Whereas there were some American female military personnel located at MASH and ASH units, they were all officers and strictly off limits to enlisted men. Well, not quite. A fellow transferred to Clearing Company from a MASH unit where he had worked in the P.X. (post exchange). As was the case with the P.X. in most units, this P.X. had a scarcity of about everything. It seemed everyone wanted a camera. Each unit received one camera per month. In order to be fair, who ever wanted it would throw his/her name in a box, and later a drawing would determine who got the camera. At the MASH was a female light colonel who desperately wanted a camera. She came into the P.X. one day and told this fellow that if he would see to it that her name was drawn for the camera, that he could have sex with her. He said she was middle aged and not too attractive, "but heck, I wasn't going to pass up an opportunity like that." She got the camera and she remained true to her word. In spite of all the change going on round about us, it would appear that there are at least two things that haven't changed: l) the way of a man with a maid and 2) the way of a maid with a man.

That sexual liaisons were formed between female and male officers is a foregone conclusion. Rank has its privileges. However, for the enlisted man, the only females available were the prostitutes who frequented the area. One evening I drove over to Division Headquarters to deliver the weekly report to the Division Surgeon's Office. Some miles to the rear of

Division Headquarters was a MASH. Now Army regulation stated that American female military personnel were to get no closer to the front line than the MASH. Obviously, then, there were no nurses at Clearing Company. As I approached the turn off to Division Headquarters, several Jeeps loaded with nurses were coming from the opposite direction and they too turned off on the road to Division Headquarters. Seems that when it came to the women fraternizing with the officers, the regulation was waived. Since they had already disobeyed regulations, why couldn't they also come to Clearing Company and fraternize with us? We too needed to have some interaction with American females. The "why" is not hard to answer. We had nothing to offer them. Division Headquarters was top heavy with brass. In addition to having a good time, and if they played their cards right, they might get a promotion, a trip to Tokyo or even some expensive gift. We at Clearing Company could give them nothing. So why would they want to fraternize with us even though we needed it as much as did the officers? And not to be forgotten was the proscription denying fraternizing between enlisted men and female officers. Although as just pointed out, that too could be waived. Looking back at this incident, I believe there is some good sociology here, something that needs to be researched. There are several examples that fit the model just described. It seems that in a situation where females are scarce, as they were in Korea, it is only the powerful males that have access to them. The weaker males can only sit by and dream. Isn't there a kind of parallel in the animal kingdom? For example, isn't it the biggest and strongest elk that collects the harem? Surely the officers weren't the biggest and strongest physically, but in modern day parlance, they were the most powerful. If power is defined as wealth, rank, position, etc., they had ready access to the few females in the group while the less powerful males were denied access to them. And the fact is women are attracted to powerful men.

Sending men on R.&.R. to Japan must have been a real agony for the military. I believe I am correct in saying that of all government bureaucracies, the military is the most conservative. The military had to recognize that while in Japan a sizeable majority of the men would spend their time with prostitutes expending the pent up sexual energy that had been building for seven long months. And of course, this is precisely what they did-not all of them, of course. More than one friend, after returning to Clearing Company from Japan, told me that what they saw of Tokyo or Kyoto was primarily the four walls of a bedroom.

I was once asked by one of my students if all G.Is. in a segregated society like Korea, thought about was sex, my response was, "Of course not. They thought about other things too, about life and death, about survival, about returning home, etc." However, it is perhaps not an exaggeration to say that for many if not most, sex was a frequent preoccupation.

Some of the men would return from Japan with V.D., however, the chances of contracting it was less in Japan than in Korea. As a rule the girls who operated out of hotels underwent regular medical checkups which curbed the spread of V.D. somewhat.

As mentioned earlier, at this time prostitution was legal in Japan. No heavy stigma was attached to Japanese prostitutes as was/is the case in the U.S. A G.I. arriving in Tokyo or Kyoto could go to a hotel that had prostitutes, be given his choice of a girl from among many, and for a charge of right around $200.00 American have the girl, the hotel room and some meals for the duration of his stay in Japan, which was usually either five or seven days.

The high V.D. rate experienced in the 45th and other divisions was a direct result of the rigid segregation of the sexes. This is not natural. It is only in celibate orders that the sexes are segregated and intercourse between males and females proscribed. The military came pretty close to this. Common sense should have told the military that in such a situation, if girls were available, whether they had V.D. or not, the men were going to avail themselves of these females. Again, I want to stress that I am not talking about every male. Of course there were those that did not engage a Korean prostitute or shack up with a prostitute in Japan. There were those who, in spite of the biological urges to do otherwise, remained faithful to their sweethearts and wives. For some, at least, remaining faithful was not easy. One afternoon while on R.&.R. I returned to my hotel room in Kyoto to take a nap. When I entered the room, a marine was sitting on his bed reading his New Testament. I greeted him and introduced myself; he did likewise. He noticed my insignia (Medics wore a caduceus on their collar) and wanted to know if I knew anything about V.D. I said I knew a little. He then proceeded to tell me that he was married, and like Bonnie and me he and his wife had vowed to remain sexually faithful to each other during their separation. His buddies, however, pressured him constantly to engage a prostitute. Finally, he gave in and did just that. The guilt was tearing him apart and he was reading his Testament for comfort and solace. We talked about symptoms of gonorrhea, and he said that at the moment he did not have a urethral discharge, however, it had only been the night before that he had had sex with the prostitute. And then he said something I have not forgotten. He said, "If I come down with gonorrhea, I am going to write my wife, tell her I was unfaithful, and that I was never coming home." I felt so darn sorry for the poor guy yet there was nothing I could do except to say that it was my experience that few fellows returning from Japan after R.&.R. came down with gonorrhea. I didn't think to ask him if he picked the prostitute up off the streets or if he got her from one of the hotels. That might have made a difference. It was my experience that the older the man and the longer he had been married, the less likely he was to have a sexual relationship with a Korean or Japanese prostitute. When talking about any kind of learned behavior, one can never generalize to all people.

When I first arrived at Clearing Company, 2nd Division, I was put in charge of a work detail. You guessed it; the detail was moving sand. I noticed that two of the men seemed out of place. They were neatly dressed and well groomed with trousers pleated, boots polished, etc. They just looked real neat. However, I hadn't been in charge of the detail more than a day or two when one of the other detail men informed me to keep my eyes on the two sharp looking men. "They're queers," he said. "It perhaps won't be too long before they may try to put the make on you." Queer was the name for homosexuals in the early fifties. Gay as a reference term for homosexual males had not yet entered the vernacular and would not for several decades. Coming from a small town in South Dakota and never knowingly having come into contact with a homosexual, I was immediately on the alert.

Now the Army took a mighty dim view of homosexuals and homosexuality and was constantly on the lookout for them. Since it was well known that these two men were gay, I was surprised they had not already been picked up. If my memory serves me correctly, back in 1954 gays were rounded up and given less than an honorable discharge.

Having heard from reliable sources, I believe there is no question that the two men were kept busy. Some men, when denied access to women for sexual purposes, will engage in what today is known as episodic or situational homosexuality. The orientation of these men is heterosexual; however, in the absence of women they resort to homosexual sex. Once women are available, they return to their former pattern of sexual expression, that of heterosexuality. The same thing is true of some men in prison populations. It should be pointed out that episodic or situational homosexuality is not unique to men alone. Some institutionalized women will also turn to homosexuality until they are able to resume a heterosexual relationship. The men may be married and don't want to be unfaithful with another woman or they may be fearful of catching V.D. There undoubtedly are any number of reasons they resort to homosexuality, but the important point is that it is episodic, occuring only occasionally, and situational, determined by the absence of women. Obviously, a situation the military brought on itself with its rigid policy of segregating the sexes. Of course, some of the men who so engaged may indeed have been homosexuals or bisexuals.

Eventually the two men were picked up, and they were not seen at Clearing Company again. However, I learned an indelible lesson about my own intolerance. While still in charge of the work detail, one day I was approached by the two men and asked, "Why are you picking on us? It is obvious you are singling us out for some of the heavier and dirtier work." Now this was after I had been informed they were gay. I hadn't realized I was "picking" on them. Gay or not, I felt badly that I let my prejudice show in that manner. And here I thought I held no prejudices towards gays. My, how easily others who are prejudiced can influence us. That is what makes prejudice so insidious, the way it can pass from one person to another, from one family member to another and from one generation to another.

So what is the answer to sex and the military? First of all, I am talking about Korea back in 1953 and 54. In a later chapter I offer a suggestion of what might have been done to ease the problem way back there almost 50 years ago. What has been done since then, I do not know. But again, and for sure, complete segregation of the sexes is not the answer. Being fully aware of the cultural and religious values of our society, of what consti-tutes moral and immoral behavior, I am more than reluctant to make any suggestions. I believe we are biologically programmed to have sex. If we weren't, most likely none of us would be here. At the same time, it is one human "drive" that can be manipulated by society as attested to by celi-bate orders, abstinence before marriage, etc. So in the past, through denial, discipline, and substitute sexual behavior such as masturbation, sexual intercourse was postponed until the cultural norm of sex within marriage was met. Of course, as current statistics reveal, this is not the case today. What about masturbation? Wouldn't that be an acceptable outlet? Not to the military which took a dim view of this behavior. In addition, it was difficult to be alone. In fact, in the military, one was seldom, if ever, alone. After marriage, engaging in sex of course, was alright. and couples were then supposed to produce children. Unfortunately, the measures often used by parents and others to cause young people to postpone sex until marriage often resulted in young people who were sexually crippled, able to reproduce, but never able to fully enjoy sex. And the sad part about this is that until recently society believed this situation was, if not ideal, at least acceptable. It is entirely possible that the attitude of the military simply reflected the attitude of the larger society, only quite a bit more so.

Earlier I suggested that the military is undoubtedly the most conservative of government bureaucracies. You may have watched the made for TV MASH episode where Hawkeye and B.J. worked feverishly to bring the movie The Moon is Blue to the unit. Sorry, but that is not the way it was. The Moon is Blue was banned throughout the 8th Army. No one got to see it in Korea. Well, perhaps I shouldn't say no one. I would imagine there were a few privileged ones who were given a private showing.

In addition, Terry Moore visited Korea and she visited Thunderbird bowl. We were told that she would be wearing her Ermine bathing suit, which at that time, I guess, made Terry Moore famous. Sure, we wanted to see Terry Moore in her Ermine bathing suit, however, it didn't happen because the 8th Army took a dim view of Terry revealing so much flesh. It is almost unbelievable that men who were expected to kill and who did kill, and who witnessed all the horrors of war, could not see Terry Moore in her Ermine bathing suit? Now tell me, is that conservative or is that conservative?

July 27th, 1953:
The Best Birthday Present Ever

The talks at Panmunjon seemed to be going better. At least that was the rumor. Of course, each time that rumor circulated, the troops got their hopes up, hoping and praying that hostilities would soon end and each time those hopes and prayers were dashed as both the war and the talks continued. The hopes and prayers were based in part on the belief that with a ceasefire and an end to hostilities, all of us would soon be going home. If ever there was a pipe dream, that was it. But why not? No one ever informed us other wise. Although talks and rumors continued, it seemed as if a ceasefire was as far off as ever.

On July 9th, Clearing Company 120th Medical Battalion made a move. I was in the advance platoon. We moved to an area closer to the front, an area that had been engaged in heavy combat with the Chinese. I can't recall how many miles the move covered but we did drive parallel to the front by truck for several hours. The area we were to occupy had apparently been the camp of a ROK outfit; it was filthy with litter everywhere. Nothing had been done to clean it up. Even worse, it was located on a slope, and we were in the midst of the rainy season. Since arriving in Korea, this was the first move in which I had been involved. It was rather hard to leave the old area, for in a way it had become home. We had just pulled into the new area when it started to pour rain. Now all of our personal gear was in the back of uncovered trucks and it got soaked. Rain or no rain, we hastily threw up a couple of tents and moved the gear under cover. In short order, the area was one muddy mess. There was mud everywhere and everyone was covered with it. As soon as the rain let up, mud or no mud, we put up the squad tents and the tents that would be used for the emergency room and the wards. We knew that casualties would be arriving shortly. I was told we were located near the village of Takkal-li, however, there was no town left and I never did find Takkal-li on the map.

The squad tents, like all the rest, were set up over mud. When we crawled onto our cots for the night, they sank deep into the mud. Since we were on a slope, the water came cascading down from the upper end of the compound. We had to dig ditches in order to divert most of the water.

We had hoped that we would be located miles from Battalion Headquarters, but it was just our luck that it was directly across the road from us. This was a bad situation for us since it meant we would constantly be subject to the crap handed out by the many officers who had nothing better to do than to harass the troops. And it started the next morning. We had barely finished erecting the squad tents when a Jeep load of brass came driving in from Battalion. The officers got out of the Jeep, even muddying their boots, walked to the end of the squad tents, took a good look, and said they were not in perfect alignment. The tents would have to be taken down and put up again; they must be in perfect alignment. I mean, this was insanity. We would soon be getting casualties, many casualties, but all those dodos could think of was that our tents were out of line. My gosh, what were they thinking of? We were at war, not on a boy scout campout…The problem was there were too many officers in Korea, who had nothing to do but sit on their asses in their hooches and dream up ways of harassing the troops.

The move was not without its satisfaction, however. Just the day before we moved, I was promoted to Corporal so that made me a Junior Non Commissioned Officer. I felt good about that.

The front line was on top of the mountain below which we were located. The sound of artillery, mortar and machine gun fire was incessant. Some of the units were so isolated that all supplies and equipment and casualties had to be taken up and brought down by helicopter. These were large copters, not the kind usually used to evacuate the wounded.

And the casualties indeed started coming most of them with serious wounds. We would do what we could to stop the bleeding or administer blood if that was necessary and then send them on to an ASH unit. We were just not set up to keep many men. Among one ambulance load of casualties was a fellow who had a penetrating wound of the side. He was bleeding internally and we needed to immediately evacuate him by helicopter to the ASH. We called for a chopper and within minutes it arrived. We didn't have service like that back at the old area. Many of the casualties were Korean but many were also G.Is. While the casualties were pouring in, new orders came down from Battalion, or I should say from across the road from Clearing Company. Now we were to fall out at 5:30 each morning for reveille and every man had to do extra detail during the day. The insanity went on.

And then on July 14th, in the midst of a torrential rain, the Chinese hit our lines at about 10:00 p.m. Until 3:00 p.m. on July 15th, there was a steady flow of casualties that came through Clearing Company. The record showed that 150 men were treated with most being sent on to a MASH or ASH unit. It appeared that our troops were caught off guard, which seemed strange since activities by the Communists had been increasing steadily. In addition to the battle casualties, quite a few men were injured when bunkers caved in and men were caught in mudslides. Without trees to hold back the earth, mudslides were common.

At this time, the heat continued to be unbearable. Earlier an old Korean gentleman told me that the heavy rains would come in July. He certainly seemed to be correct.

The Chinese offensive continued unabated. In fact, I was told it was the longest and most intensive offensive in two years. At the 120th as well as other units in the Division, every unit was being brought up to T.O.& E. (Table of Organization and Equipment.) In effect that meant each unit was being brought up to full strength both in men and equipment. A company calls for about 250 men; that is about what we now had at Clearing Company. Other units likewise had their full quota of men. The same was true of equipment; each unit received its full quota of the equipment it was supposed to have. It was the Chinese offensive and the bringing of the Company to full strength that led me to believe that if the negotiations at Panmunjon failed the allied forces were going to go on the offensive with all the firepower at its command. And, I was reminded, we had control of the skies; the Chinese had few aircraft. But, when the fighting was intense, so were the peace talks. It is possible that there was a sense among the negotiators that a ceasefire was so close that the Chinese wanted to inflict as much damage as they could on allied forces before the shooting stopped. One thing was certain. Anyone who had the audacity to call this a mere police action was daft; it was a full-scale war. I often wondered if the American people were being told the full truth about Korea. Did they even care?

One very hot day a short time later, the temperature was around 114 degrees fahrenheit with humidity about the same, I received a call to meet an incoming helicopter with two bodies aboard. It was my duty to tag the bodies and to get names, ranks and serial numbers, etc. I grabbed a Jeep and drove to the landing pad just as the chopper arrived. As soon as the door of the chopper was opened, the smell of death filled my nostrils. One of the dead was an American G.I.; the other was a Korean soldier. I helped unload the stretchers from the chopper after which it promptly took off for the front lines to bring in more dead. The body of the G.I. was lying face down. His left leg and side had been literally chewed into hamburger by an artillery shell. When I got him turned over, he was drenched in blood from head to foot. His eyes were open and he had the most startled expression on his face. His left leg was lying along side his body with his foot tucked under his armpit. His dog tag was attached to that foot with barbed wire. Since dog tags were worn around the neck, I wondered what it was doing attached to his foot. Later a buddy of his told me the dead man's last request; Write to my girl friend and tell her I died like a hero. Maybe he had a premonition of his coming death; maybe it was more of a joke. No one would ever know. He was killed at around 10:00 p.m. Because of the heat and humidity, decomposition was already setting in.

The South Korean soldier had caught a bullet in his mid section, just below the bottom of his flak jacket. His death must have been slow and agonizing since he had agony written all over his face. His right hand was hooked onto the flack jacket just above the bullet hole. I noticed the jacket had a small tear where he was grasping it. Now it may be that the tear happened earlier, but it is also possible that in his death agonies he had caused that small tear.

As with the American G.I., I got the necessary information off his body. When I was finished, both bodies were loaded on the back of the Jeep and taken to graves registration. I was surprised to see only one person was in charge, especially since there were a considerable number of bodies coming in from the various regiments. The fellow at graves registration got out two green rubberized body bags, and we placed the bodies in them. Then I asked him, "Where do you want the bodies?" "Let's just carry them out a distance from the tent so I don't have to put up with the odor," he said. So we placed them away from the tent in heat that was well over 100 degrees.

As I drove back to Clearing Company, I pondered over what had just transpired. Two men were dead, one of them horribly shattered; but for a few friends, no one cared, no one shed any tears for them. The G.I. had died on a battlefield far from home, fighting a senseless war. I say senseless because there was no intention of winning it. As I was to learn later, that decision was made sometime during the summer of 1951. In fact, later the Korean War became known as the only war, up to that point, engaged in by America without the intent to win. Vietnam turned out to be much the same. When alive, the average G.I. didn't amount to much, but when life was extinguished, he was nothing more than dead flesh. The best that could be done for him was to put him in a zippered body bag and lay his body out in the burning heat. For the G.I., and most likely the Korean as well, when their folks got the news, it would be a far different reaction.

One thing I could not understand is why mothers, primarily mothers, didn't rise up in an absolute rage. That G.I. lying on the stretcher with his body torn apart by an artillery round, was some mother's son. She had conceived him, carried him in her womb for nine months. She had suffered through the pain of his birth, nestled him to her breast as she fed him, and soothed his bruises when he was a little boy. She had comforted him when he shared with her the frustrations of his teen years, agonized over the prospects of his being drafted, and tried to keep a positive demeanor, for his sake, when he left for basic training. She had felt the icy fingers of fear when she learned he was going to Korea, and hoped and prayed that he would survive to return to her in one piece. And now, the best the Army could do for him was to put him in a rubber bag and lay his decomposing body out in the unbearable hot sun. At some point his remains would be sealed in a casket, and she would never know any of the details of his death. There was no one to weep for that son she loved, no one to really care that he had died such an awful death. Perhaps the Army should have hired professional Korean mourners, if such existed, to at least foster the pretense that there was sadness in his death.

I couldn't help but remember the death of another G.I. One morning his body was brought to Clearing Company. He had been killed in a truck accident. None of the graves registration units I called wanted to take him. In the first place he should not have been brought to Clearing Company. Since he was killed instantly, he should have been taken directly to graves registration. He lay there on the floor covered with a blanket for almost five hours before I found one graves registration outfit that would take him. It all had something to do with filling out the proper papers.

I wondered if one had to become immune to the emotions that usually accompany death since there was so much of it. In my own case, I know that after a time, I became hardened to it. If I had grieved over every body that came through Clearing Company, I would have exhausted my grief in very short order. But, it still didn't seem right. When that day ended, we had 11 sheets of paper filled with names of the casualties, both the dead and the wounded.

On the 26th of July a report came over the radio. In my letter to Bonnie I wrote, "Today at approximately 4:30 p.m., a news flash came over the radio that tomorrow at 10:00 a.m., the signing of the ceasefire will take place." At long last the many, many prayers for peace had been answered. In a very short time, the killing would stop. I experienced a great sense of relief. No more deaths, no more casualties. Now everyone could make plans that had a chance of being realized, or at least they wouldn't be dashed due to death on the battlefield.

Clearing Company 120th Medical Battalion.
Location when the ceasefire went into effect. Do the Squad Tents look out of line to you?

July 27th will always be a very special day for me for several reasons. First, it is the date of my birth. Second, my paternal grandfather, a man I was very close to, died on July 27th, 1944, and now, the Korean war would come to an end on July 27th, 1953. No birthday rolls around without giving thought to these momentous events.

As stated on the news report, at 10:20 a.m., on the morning of July 27th, the ceasefire was signed and 12 hours later it went into effect. And yet, during those 12 hours we had many casualties come to and through Clearing Company. The Chinese were not going to let up until the very end. What an irony. A ceasefire had been signed and yet many would die in the 12 hours before it would go into effect. It had to be sheer hell for the men on the front line, hoping and praying that they just might make it through the next 12 hours

At 10:20 p.m. the guns fell silent. In a way it was eerie. In fact for a couple of nights I could not sleep; it was too quiet. Since my arrival in Korea, each night there would be a serenade of mortars, artillery and machine gun fire. Now all was quiet on the eastern and western fronts. It is hard to put in writing the inexpressible joy that accompanied this silence and the belief that the shooting would not start up again. And yet, I had to remember that it was only a ceasefire, not an armistice nor a conditional or unconditional surrender. A ceasefire could be broken at any time. It should have been a time for celebration, but the Army, with all of its screwball ideas, had something else up its sleeve. As crazy as it may seem, we, the men of 120th Clearing Company and, I imagine, men throughout the Division, had to sign a pledge saying that we would not celebrate. At any rate, it was a very happy 22nd birthday. At least now I had a much better chance of having many more returns of the day.

What followed was utter chaos. Immediately we were to withdraw (as were the Chinese and North Koreans) 1000 yards behind the M.L.R. (Main Line of Resistance or front line.) This area soon became known as the Demilitarized Zone. Frantically we tore down the medical tents and Quonsets, the personnel tents and the control post. Taking down tents and Quonset huts was no big deal but packing up all of the medical instruments, etc., was a delicate and time-consuming process. At last everything was loaded and we moved out. Our new location was a delight. It was a level area away from the mountains and located next to a rather sizeable flowing stream. In addition, there was a rather large stand of trees scattered about. Since trees of any kind were a rarity, we considered ourselves lucky indeed.

Immediately we began setting up Clearing Company, 120th Medical Battalion. The first tents and quonsets to go up were the hospital wards and quonsets. We had wounded with us and men who had been hospitalized for reasons other than shrapnel or bullet wounds. In addition, in short order, we had to be ready for the sick and injured coming from throughout the Division. And I must say, we did a commendable job. In a relatively short time we were ready to receive the sick and injured. The living quarters for the troops would have to wait for another day.

We were just getting settled in when our company commander called us all together and told us to cease what we were doing. Division Headquarters had another idea about where we were to be located. In short, we were to pull up stakes and move again. Were we discouraged? You bet we were. For once we had a nice area and the task of setting up Clearing Company was about complete. Now it would have to all be undone and we would lose the delightful settings. It seems that an entire regiment wanted our area, and the General gave it to them. It made no difference that we were about finished setting up the wards, squad tents, etc. Beyond any doubt, a regiment carried a lot more clout than a mere medical unit did. For some reason or other, Clearing Companies, in general, seemed to rate rather low on the totem pole. This was not only true of the 45th Division but of the 2nd Division as well. They were low on the totem pole, that is, until the casualties poured in, then they rated number one.

At this time our company commander was a doctor, not a career officer. Along with the enlisted men, he had his fill of it. "Men," he said, "Stop what you are doing and at 21 hundred hours, let's meet by the creek and have a party and then, let's all take tomorrow off." As parties go, it wasn't much, however, there was a good supply of beer, Japanese beer, and not the green American beer that at best was difficult to down. The Japanese beer came in liter-sized bottles and was preferred by most men to the

American beer. Each bottle had its own straw jacket with a small woven handle, which I thought was unique. The party lasted as long as the beer.

The next a.m. there was no reveille, no need to fall out in formation. We just goofed off. The stream was clear so most of us went swimming among unexploded mortar rounds, unfired rifle rounds, 50 caliber machine gun rounds and other small military hardware. Apparently some unit had discarded this hardware when it was given the word to move, or it could have found its way into the stream earlier in the war when that piece of real estate was being fought over. For one day, at least, we at Clearing Company were free from military restraints.

On the following morning, however, the move commenced. Down came the hospital wards and whatever else had been erected two days earlier. As the tents and quonsets were being loaded into trucks, several trays loaded with medical instruments were knocked to the ground and scattered about. As we stooped to pick up the scalpels, hemostats, etc., the doctors said, "Just let it be where it is, we do not have time to pick it all up. When we arrive at our new location, we will requisition new instruments." And that is what we did; we left all that expensive equipment lying on the ground. Among the scattered instruments was a complete field kit. One of the medics, who was not about to leave the field kit behind, picked it up and stashed it with his gear. So far as I know, he was successful in sending it home. Perhaps he was the only smart one since even in 1953 medical instruments were expensive.

Other than a move to the M.L.R., which was an ecological disaster with the ground everywhere torn up and littered with debris, our move this time had to be to one of the most God forsaken pieces of real estate in Korea. It was on a hillside that had been churned up by artillery fire and completely devoid of any plant life. In addition, it was a mud hole. A bulldozer was brought to the area, and the dirt was rearranged in such a way that flat areas were created. I was standing around watching the bulldozer moving dirt when suddenly a full case of hand grenades rolled out in front of the blade. Of course, the bulldozer shut down until a demolition crew could come and remove the grenades. It was on these flat areas that the hospital tents and quonsets, the living quarters for troops and officers, the control post, the supply tent, etc., were erected. And it was here that the personnel of Clearing Company spent the next five months. And for the next five months, it remained a mud hole. Nothing we did could change that.

DEATH TAKES NO HOLIDAY

It was September and I had been in Korea for seven months. Other than ambulance trips to nearby ASH and MASH hospitals, I had not been out of the company area. I needed to get away and to do so badly. After awhile the tedium gets depressing. Although Seoul was not too far to the south, so far there were no opportunities to go there. However, after seven months I was eligible for R.&.R. to Japan. But as with everything else, I was put on a waiting list. I made frequent inquiries as to when my name would come up for the trip to Japan. I don't recall how many times I was told, "It will be soon." But it seemed that "soon" would never come. Fellows from the 120th were returning, primarily from Tokyo, with tales of great times, entertainment of every kind and of beautiful Japanese girls. It had been seven months since I last saw a woman other than the prostitutes that occasionally passed through the company. I did see Korean farm women from time to time, however, they appeared very plain and unattractive. Having said that, a word of explanation is in order. These were farm women who constantly wore traditional clothing, either a pair of trousers and shirt or a short jacket like blouse and a long skirt that came just below the breasts. They wore no makeup and there was no variation in hairstyles. This is not meant to be critical; these farmers had all they could do just to survive. There was no money for cosmetics, and even if there was, it is doubtful the women would have used them. Most likely there were no cosmetics to be purchased. These were a traditional people far removed both physically and psychologically from the amenities of the industrial societies of the West. Yet, once introduced, it is amazing how quickly Western ideas and ideals replaced the traditional ones, which the Koreans had adhered to for centuries. So, to hear tell of the beautiful girls in Japan couldn't help but quicken the heartbeat and increase eagerness to be going on R.&.R.

I must add that from time to time, U.S.O. shows were brought to the Company amphitheater and these almost always included a few women. They certainly did serve as a reminder of what American women looked like. But, as a rule, they proved to be a problem. Ours was a military unit staffed entirely by men. Suddenly there were women in the compound, women who needed to take showers and use the toilets. When they went to the showers an armed guard always accompanied them. I found this highly insulting since the implication was clear: with women in the compound, the men were not to be trusted since they might go berserk and rape them. Just another example of how the enlisted man was viewed as incapable of making independent judgment. I never did hear of a G.I. going berserk and attempting to rape one of the U.S.O. women. Of course they were off limits to all enlisted men. I can't say the same about the officers. It is to he remembered that officers were a different breed of cats. All in all, because of the disruptions they caused, I do believe we would have been better off had the U.S.O. shows not come to Clearing Company. Furthermore, seldom did we have a show which provided us with top-notch entertainment.

And then one day, it was my turn. Ken Worthington, Company Clerk, told me that my name had come down on the R.&.R. list. I would be leaving Clearing Company on the 22nd of September for seven days in Kyoto. I would be the only one from the 120th to go to Kyoto; others going on R.&.R. would be going to Tokyo.

When the morning of the 22nd arrived, I, along with half dozen other fellows from the 120th, climbed in the back of an open truck. There were no paved roads in the Korean backcountry, which meant that in short order we were covered with a heavy layer of dust. It hardly paid to take a shower the night before or to put on a clean uniform. At Ch'unch'on I processed for R.&.R. to Kyoto. The processing didn't amount to much, largely a final check to see that I had all the necessary documents identifying who I was and that I was authorized to leave the 120th for Kyoto. In Ch'unch'on, I again boarded a train. For some reason or other, all of the trains I rode in Korea, and that included several, moved very slowly. An uninterrupted drive from Clearing Company to Seoul by truck would take about two hours, given the condition of the roads. The trip with the stop over in Ch'unch'on, and the slow train ride would take the better part of the day.

When the train finally reached the outskirts of Seoul, it stopped several miles from the K-16 Airstrip, the take off point for Japan. It seemed rather strange and even a bit exciting to be in a city once again. There was much hustle and bustle and considering that South Korea was on a war time footing, considerable traffic on the highways. The train was parked just a short distance from what must have been a major transportation artery in the Seoul area.

As soon as the train stopped, the area was besieged with little urchins selling trinkets, pornographic pictures and even some beer. The trinkets were made from brass shell casings that had been scrounged from nearby firing ranges. The Koreans were ingenious; they made the most attractive items out of brass. I bought a couple of folding double picture frames for the equivalent of a dollar or two; they were heavily engraved with Korean scenes. I still use those frames today.

I was enjoying all this activity when I noticed a woman and two small boys standing very close to the train car I was occupying. Obviously, the woman was the mother of the two boys. I guessed her age at around 40 or at most the early forties. It was darn hard to guess the correct age of Korean women. They seemed to age rapidly and I would usually guess their age to be considerably older than they actually were.

I wanted to get a picture of the three of them so I stepped down on the steps of the car, took a meter reading and raised my camera to my eye. Now on the far side of the nearby highway, I noticed a little boy standing by himself looking in our direction. He couldn't have been more than four or five years old. With my camera raised to my eye, the woman and the two boys, the highway and the little fellow on the far side of the highway were all within the camera viewfinder. At that precise moment, a scene of horror unfolded before my eyes. The little fellow on the far side of the highway stepped off the curb into the line of traffic and was immediately struck by a truck loaded with heavy water bottles. The truck passed over his little body, and he lay very still on the road. The woman with the two boys turned just after the truck passed over the body of the little boy, and with a scream ran across the highway oblivious to the oncoming traffic and the danger in which she was placing herself. She grabbed the little body and carried it to the curb. Immediately she sat down, laid the broken little body across her legs and began to pound on it with her fists. She did this for a few moments, and then she laid the body down and ran at the truck driver who had stopped and was standing at the back end of his truck. When she reached him, she commenced pounding him on the chest, all the while screaming. Then she ran back to the body of what obviously was her son, sat down on the curb, picked him up, held him tightly and swayed back and forth, moaning very audibly. She continued to do this for some time when finally three men standing close by on the sidewalk walked over to her. One took the body of her son and laid it in the gutter; the other two lifted her to her feet kicking and struggling and led her away from the tragic scene of the death of her son.

Death never takes a holiday

I was so transfixed by all of this that I suddenly realized that the camera was still to my eye, and I had witnessed this entire episode through the viewfinder of my camera. I couldn't recall if I had tripped the shutter or not. I had seen plenty of death, but this was something else. I was speechless. I went back into the train car and just sat down, finding it hard to believe that I had really witnessed the death of the little boy. As I looked out the window and across the highway, the little body was still plainly visible. Shortly, a man carrying a straw mat walked over to the body and covered it. I assumed that leaving it there either had something to do with Korean culture, or it had to remain there until the police arrived. However, I never did see any police.

A half hour later, trucks arrived from the K-16 Airstrip. We boarded and, as we drove to the airstrip, we passed the scene of the accident. The little body was still lying in the gutter, and was still covered by the straw mat. The truck, loaded with large water bottles, must have weighed many tons. This was obvious by the damage done to that young body. Body fluids, blood and tissue had squirted out almost to the center of the highway. Needless to say, witnessing the death of the little boy put a heavy damper on my enthusiasm for R.&.R. I could not push what I had seen out of my mind. I still did not know whether or not I had pressed the shutter release on my camera. When in Kyoto, I had the film developed. One of the pictures showed the mother just turning to look at her son who was already lying dead on the highway just a short distance behind the truck.

When I returned to Clearing Company after my seven days in Kyoto, I asked Willie, one of our interpreters, why the mother, after laying the broken little body on her lap, pounded it with her fists? His response was that she was trying to pound life back into the body. Poor, poor woman. She had the rest of her life to agonize over leaving her child on the far side of the highway while she and her two other sons came across to the parked train.

The memory of that mother trying to pound life into her small child is permanently etched in my mind. I can't forget it and from time to time it pushes to the forefront and haunts me. Why did she leave the child on the far side of the road? Had he perhaps been sleeping? What was she doing by the train? Her sons weren't selling any trinkets. All unanswered questions.

This was to have been a happy occasion for me, one I had looked forward to for months and now it was marred by the memory of that tragic event in Seoul. How true it is that death never takes a holiday.

SETSUKO

I had been in Korea for seven long months and was yearning to be somewhere else. With the signing of the ceasefire, R.&.R. was extended from five to seven days. I was about due for R.&.R., however, I had a problem. Most of the fellows from Clearing Company spent their R.&.R. in Tokyo. I too wanted to go to Tokyo, however, I was told in no uncertain terms that if I went to Tokyo I would not return a virgin. Now it is a rare occurrence when a man can be forced to have sex against his will and that wasn't my concern. My concern was the constant pressure I would be under to get myself a prostitute and do what so many of the fellows did. What they did was to take advantage of a package deal; a girl, a hotel room, and three meals a day for seven days at a cost of just under $200.00 American. I didn't want that kind of pressure. Although my resolve was strong I was only human and badly in need of female companionship. In addition, I had been told that most of the prostitutes were attractive. So, when I was told they would see to it that I got "laid," they were saying in effect that they would put me into a situation where it would be next to impossible to say no. After all, I was 22 years old and like most 22-year-old men who had seen only a few women in seven months, mostly Korean prostitutes, testosterone was coursing through my blood stream in excessive amounts

Earlier, while engaged in a discussion with tent mates about sex, sexual exploits and women, a good "friend" wanted to know if Bonnie and I had experienced intercourse with each other? I had told him earlier that we were engaged. I said "No." Then he wanted to know if I had ever had sex with a woman. Again I said, "No," and that was a mistake. What I should have said is "Buddy, its none of your damn business." The reaction was one of disbelief. Those tent mates made it sound as if every 22 year old

105

was an old hand at intercourse. I knew differently, however, I paid dearly in humiliation for that admission. In a short time it seemed that everyone in Clearing Company knew it and, of course, there were a couple of wise guys who wouldn't let them forget that fact. Now I am sure there were plenty of other fellows at the 120th who had not engaged in sex. Unlike me, however, they were smart enough not to admit it. And so the decision was made that, "If Waltner goes with us to Tokyo, he will not be coming back a virgin."

What to do? I wanted to go to Tokyo. The only other city on the roster for this go around of R.&.R. was Kyoto, and no one had signed up for that city. If I went to Kyoto, I would be going alone. To say the least, that really didn't appeal to me.

After meeting and falling in love with Bonnie, we made a vow that we would remain virgins and that she would be my first sex partner and I hers. In addition, sex out of wedlock, either side, was not a part of my moral and value system. Again, I am sure I was not alone in this. It is to be remembered this was 1953 and not 2000. As I was to discover later, there were a lot of liars among the young men. I signed up for Kyoto and anticipated a lonely seven days in Japan.

On the morning of September 22, I jumped into the back of a truck, rode to Ch'unch'on, where I processed for R&R, and then boarded a train for the K-16 Airstrip. It was late afternoon before the plane took off for a three-hour flight to Kobe, Japan. Again I had to process for my stay in Japan. In addition, I was issued a couple of class B uniforms (khakis). Instead of low quarter shoes, I would be wearing the boots that accompanied me from Korea.

After processing for the stay in Japan, I sat down to the most delicious meal I had eaten in seven months. There was real American beefsteak and all the trimmings plus the best milk I had ever consumed in spite of the fact that it was reconstituted from powdered milk.

By now the hour was late, and though I could have left for Kyoto, I opted to spend the night at the military compound in Kobe. A good number of fellows made the same decision. There were many other men representing all the divisions in Korea as well as supporting units. Most of the men had at least one buddy from their unit in Korea. I was alone and feeling more lonely by the minute.

The next morning, the morning of the 23rd, I finally had my fast train ride. I boarded a train in Kobe, and in an hour I stepped off the train in Kyoto. A short distance from the depot was the Rakuyo hotel, a hotel that had been leased by the American government for use by men coming to Kyoto from Korea for R.&.R. I grabbed my duffel bag (a duffel bag was an omnipresent piece of equipment) and walked to the hotel. As soon as I entered the outer lobby of the Rakuyo, I saw the beautiful girls I had been told about. Of course, they were prostitutes looking for a pickup. In 1953 prostitution in Japan was legal. The girls were permitted to enter the outer lobby of the hotel but could go no farther. Prostitutes or no prostitutes, I thought they were beautiful. They were so small and petite and all of them had very dark hair. Perhaps gentlemen prefer blondes but this G.I. preferred girls with dark hair, the darker the better. It was not easy walking past them since picking one up would have been such an easy thing to do.

The Rakuyo was a very large and nice hotel. I guess there was no such thing as a private room. I was assigned a room with six beds; however, I don't believe there was a single night when all beds were occupied. Many of the men picked up a prostitute and stayed with her, returning to the hotel only to clean up and change into a fresh suit of clothing. The services at the hotel were terrific with laundry being done every day. If my memory serves me correctly, the hotel room cost me $7.00 per day. In addition, all meals could be had at the hotel; fifteen cents for breakfast, twenty-five cents for lunch and thirty-five cents for the evening meal. I certainly couldn't beat those prices at a restaurant, butI didn't want to stick around the hotel just so I could have very good and cheap meals. I wanted to see Kyoto. That meant I would have to find a restaurant that served Western food. Part of the processing for R.&.R. that took place in Kobe involved where and what we should eat. "Eat only Western food," I was told, "since the Japanese, like the Koreans, fertilize their fields with human excrement and if you eat native food, you are running the risk of getting intestinal parasites." So, I ate Western food and I didn't get dysentery, but I also didn't take advantage of the opportunity to eat native Japanese dishes. I regret that and I really don't think the risk of dysentery was that great.

I believe it was my first day and night in Kyoto when the area was hit by a typhoon. All G.Is. in the Rakuyo were ordered to stay in the hotel. I didn't need the order since the last place I wanted to be was out of doors. Oh yes, I was not free of military control. It seemed the city was swarming with M.Ps., and I was told I could be stopped for the slightest infraction of the rules and if the infraction was serious enough, R.&.R. would be terminated. There was no getting out of the Army that was for sure.

By morning the typhoon had passed and though it inflicted considerable damage on Nara and Kobe, the damage in Kyoto was slight.

Before I left Korea, one of my friends who had spent his R.&.R. in Kyoto gave me the address of a restaurant that served Western food. In addition, it was connected to a public bath, a place where I could get seven months of Korean crud steamed out of my body. That I was looking forward to. So, without eating breakfast at the hotel, I hailed a taxi, gave the driver the piece of paper on which the address of the restaurant and bathhouse were written, and had the ride of my life. One has not experienced real driving until sitting behind a Japanese cab driver. At least that was the case in 1953. Many of the streets in Kyoto were narrow and without sidewalks. Of course, the people walked in the streets. When the cab turned up one of those narrow streets, the cabbie laid on the horn and went barreling down the street. Why he didn't hit several people I'll never know. Good driver, good pedestrians or both.

I was relieved to arrive at the restaurant without having been party to an accident. I forget what the charge was, a few yen at most. Back in 1953, the yen to dollar exchange rate was 360 yen to one dollar. In effect, the taxi ride cost me nothing. I believe the tip I gave him amounted to more than the ride. I walked into the small restaurant, and quickly became aware that I was the only G.I. in the place. I got the impression that it was not frequented often by G.Is. I was correct. Come to think of it, it was a kind of out of the way place not located anywhere near the main Kyoto business district. In addition, when I walked through the door, the waitresses stopped what they were doing and looked at me as if to say, "What in the world are you doing here?" Nonetheless, a young woman came up to me, made a slight bow and led me to a table. Now what? They had no menu printed in English, and the young woman who took me to the table couldn't speak English. She made a few gestures and left. By this time I was beginning to feel pretty conspicuous and foolish. I wished I had eaten at the hotel since all of the waitresses there could speak English, however, I did not want to spend seven days at the Rakuyo. Because of the typhoon of the day before, I was already into my second day of R.&.R. In short order, however, a different young woman approached my table and informed me that she could speak English and that she would tell me what was on the menu. I told her I was interested in Western food and in a very short time I placed my order for breakfast.

To say the least, the place was not exactly bulging at the seams with patrons. To the few who were eating there, I was a curiosity. The discomfort level began to rise. When the waitress brought my breakfast, she placed it in front of me and left. However, she must have sensed my discomfort, and in a few moments she was back at my table. Blushing deeply, she asked if she could sit down. Of course she could, I was most happy to have her do so. I needed to talk to someone. I tried to put her at erase by starting a conversation. She told me her name was Setsuko Shinohara. The Shin sounded Japanese but the Ohara sounded Irish. Setsuko was no Irish girl, to be sure. I told her my name was Dick. We repeated each other's names a couple of times and then we were ready to talk. Setsuko was a petite little gal, and in my eyes was very cute. Most of our early conversation was about me. "Was I a G.I. from Korea on R.&.R.? Where was I staying? How did I find the restaurant? Was I with some other G.Is from my outfit in Korea." She was surprised to hear I was alone. I asked her a few questions about herself. She worked at the restaurant to help support her mother. I got the impression that her father was no longer living, a casualty of the war perhaps. I also got the impression that money was a scarce commodity for Setsuko and her mother. And, we talked about other things. One thing was certain; the two of us hit it off from the start. I told her that after I finished eating, I wanted to take a steam bath and then a hot bath. She knew all about soaking out the Korean crud. She had heard it before from other G.Is. on R.&.R. When breakfast was over, she called two young women to the table, and speaking Japanese, I guess she told them what I wanted. Setsuko told me to follow them.

Dear Setsuko

First the girls put me into a steam cabinet. When I was "locked" in, they left. At first it felt wonderful. But as time went by, it got too hot and I found it difficult to breathe. One of the girls poked her head into the room, and somehow I let her know that I had had enough of the steam cabinet. I must have looked pretty frantic since both girls rushed over to the cabinet and got me out of it. From the steam cabinet they led me to a small stool and signaled that I should sit down. All I had to cover myself with was a small washcloth and that wasn't doing a very good job so I discarded it. I figured the girls did this so often that they really weren't interested in what this G.I. looked like naked as a jaybird. While on the stool, they soaped me up real good and then rinsed me off. This didn't take long. Next they led me to a tub full of crystal clear steaming water. They gestured I should get in. The steam rising from the water concerned me since I knew it was hot. Nonetheless, I slowly lowered myself into that tub and for a moment I thought I was going to be scalded. However, gradually my body got used to it. I have often wondered, just what was the temperature of the water? When I was settled into the tub, the girls again left the room and I soaked and soaked. I then understood what my buddies meant when they said that one of those Japanese baths will soak all of the Korean crud right out of you. Japanese, like many Orientals, believe that taking a bath in America is a very unclean process because after Americans wash themselves they lie back and soak in the very dirt they removed in the first place. I imagine there is some truth in what they say. By taking what is equivalent to a shower before climbing into the tub of hot water, the body is already clean. Therefore, by soaking in the tub, the dirt is not re-absorbed by the body; the water is as crystal clear when one crawls out of the tub as when he/she crawled in. It is one of those interesting cultural differences.

After a time the two girls returned and motioned for me to get out of the tub. I stepped out and was given a huge towel with which to dry myself. It wasn't over yet, however. Next I was led to a table and again, through sign language, signaled to crawl onto the table and to lie on my stomach. I had heard about Japanese girls giving a massage by walking all over one's body and legs. That is exactly what they did and did it ever feel good. They used the toes and heels of their feet like magic. Without any doubt, it was the best massage I ever had. Come to think of it, it was the only massage I ever had.

After the massage, I dressed and went back into the restaurant and sat at a table. Setsuko came over and I ordered a beer. I asked her what she would like to drink, and she said that she wanted nothing. However, I persisted and she came back to the table with the beer and some kind of bottled soft drink. In the next few days she would drink a lot of the pop or whatever it was. Back in 1953, excellent beer in Japan was not put up in 12 ounce bottles but more like liter sized bottles.

While we were drinking our beverages, Setsuko asked me, "what are you going to do?" I told her I was going to take a taxi to down town Kyoto. Blushing, and with downcast eyes, she then asked me if I would like her to be my guide while I was in Kyoto? She couldn't go with me today, however, she would make arrangements to go with me during the afternoon and evening hours for the remainder of my stay in Kyoto. I told her I would be most happy if she would show me the sights of Kyoto. How lucky could I get. Here I arrived in Kyoto concerned that for seven days I was going to be one lonely fellow and now I had an attractive young Japanese woman who was going to show me points of interest in the city.

That evening I did go to down town Kyoto. Instead of taking a taxi, I walked. The distance from the Rakuyo Hotel to down town Kyoto must have been close to three miles, however, I found it a most enjoyable walk. After the typhoon had passed the weather had cleared and the evening was beautiful. As I was enjoying my walk, two girls and a fellow came out of a building I was passing. One girl asked, "Hey G.I., would you like to have me? Cost you only $5.00." I said no thanks and continued walking. They followed and kept bugging me to shack up with one or both girls, $5.00 for each. I again thanked them for the offer and again declined, however, they persisted following along as I walked toward Kyoto.

Finally, in exasperation, one of the girls asked, ""What's a matter G.I., you queer?" Queer, me queer? Now that was a laugh. Had they only known how much my body was saying, "Yes, yes, yes, do it." However, I was well aware that it was girls like these who were usually infected with gonorrhea. I couldn't help but compare the two girls with the girls waiting in the outer lobby of the hotel. They never said a word. If sex was going to be negotiated, it was the G.I. who had to make the first move. In addition, whereas the girls in the hotel were dressed neat as a pin, the street girls were wearing jeans and a plain shirt.

The next day, at noon, I met Setsuko at the restaurant, and we took a taxi to downtown Kyoto. We must have made an interesting looking pair, Setsuko barely reaching five feet and I six feet in height. She took me to many places, places that I do not believe I would have visited had she not been with me. We went to the complex where girls were trained to be Geishas. It was an imposing building, but we did not have access to it. Setsuko went to great pains to inform me that contrary to the common view, true Geisha girls were not high class, high priced prostitutes but girls trained in the art of entertainment. One evening, a number of them put on a program at the hotel. At the time Setsuko and I were in downtown Kyoto and I missed the performance. Had I seen this performance I could speak more directly to the kind of entertainment they provided. I believed Setsuko so for me the issue was cleared up. Geishas were not prostitutes.

One evening we were eating supper as usual in a restaurant that served American food. I ordered something American while Setsuko ordered a Japanese dish. I was fascinated by what Setsuko ordered. She was brought a heaping plate of steamed rice shaped like a volcano. At the top was a depression. In addition her order included a raw egg. The rice was extremely hot. Setsuko cracked the egg and dumped its contents into the depression in the mound of rice. It was the hot rice, that cooked the egg. At the time, that wasn't too appealing to me but I wish I had tried it. She laughed at my amazement that the rice could cook the egg. Setsuko laughed a lot. She said it was good and in spite of my reservations I have no doubt that it was.

As we were eating, several young Japanese men entered the restaurant. They sat at a table some distance from ours; however, we were clearly the focus of their attention. I could see they were getting increasingly agitated and began to get an uneasy feeling that I was in trouble. They got up from their table and walked to ours. There were three of them. They spoke to Setsuko and whatever they said it was said in anger. They would gesture toward me and occasionally throw me a glance. Setsuko remained calm through their tirade. When they finished talking, she replied to them in a quiet and calm voice. What she said must have satisfied them. Casting me an angry glance, they left. I asked Setsuko, "What that was all about?" She told me that they were very angry that a Japanese girl (other than a prostitute) would have anything to do with an American soldier. They were angry with her for dating me and angry with me for being an American. Setsuko said they threatened to beat up on me, but she was able to convince them that ours was a respectable relationship and not a sexual one. I could have reached over and hugged her right then and there. Now in my youth, I was pretty husky, but there is no way I could have handled those three fellows had a fight broken out and even worse, had we fought, most likely the M.Ps. would have been called and I would have ended up heading back to Korea before my R.&.R. was up. I tried putting myself in their position and was able to sympathize with them. I could imagine my reaction had the situation been reversed. Japanese men dating American girls. I too would have been angry especially when just a few years earlier, the Japanese had been our enemies. Of course, it was not hypothetical. Americans had been their enemies.

One evening after dinner, Setsuko announced that she was going to show me something that most likely very few G.Is. had the opportunity to see. By now our relationship was developing into something a bit more than purely platonic. I don't see how it could have been otherwise. We had been together the better part of three days. Of course, I couldn't help but be aware of the way her feelings were changing toward me, and I was acutely aware of how my own feelings were undergoing change. I often felt the desire to reach out for her. I knew that from this point on, I was going to have to watch my emotions carefully. That wouldn't be easy. I have always liked women, I enjoy their companionship. I was lonely and so much in need of female companionship. Setsuko recognized this and provided me with that and much more. She recognized in me a very lonely young man and she, so to speak, took me under her wing. But now our platonic relationship was developing into something more. I had to steel myself against it even though, in the short term, I knew it wasn't fair to Setsuko. I was in love with Bonnie. I was engaged and would be married shortly after arriving home. Plans for the wedding were progressing nicely. Falling in love with a Japanese girl would have been a dead end. This had happened to many of the fellows, and it was almost impossible to get the military's permission to marry. Getting the girl to the states presented additional obstacles. Even if the girl was cleared to immigrate to the U.S. the procedure was complicated. In addition, the Japanese did not look fondly on their girls marrying American boys. So far as that goes, the Koreans also took a very dim view of amalgamation, and the military was even more adamant that G.Is. not marry Korean girls. Keith Lassiter, a buddy from the 120th, fell in love with a Korean girl and she with him. He had absolutely no luck with military officials. Finally in total exasperation, he decided to hell with them. He would go home to the States, get his discharge and then return to Korea to marry the girl. As I understood, that is exactly what he did. Given the environment today, it is hard to imagine the amount of prejudice held by the military toward girls of Japanese and Korean nationality. In all fairness, I should point out that when all obstacles were finally overcome and marriage and immigration did take place, many of those marriages did not work out.

We had turned off the main street of Kyoto and walked some distance before we came to the most delightful park. It was the kind of Japanese Park one often saw in pictures. There were plants of many kinds and small streams of water flowing from many sources. Arched bridges formed walk-ways across the streams. The walkways were dimly lit with Japanese lanterns and to make the romantic setting complete, soft Japanese music was piped in throughout the park. It was idyllic and very romantic. Setsuko and I sat down on one of the small benches next to a small stream, and it was obvious both of us were taken with the romantic atmosphere of the park. She snuggled close up against me, and I put my arms around her and held her tightly. We talked very little, but when we did, it was in hushed tones. I have no idea how long we stayed that way when finally Setsuko broke the mood by announcing that she had to go home for she knew her mother would be worrying about her. Both of us were reluctant to break the spell that had settled over us, and we did not want to leave that secluded haven. But that is just what we did. I don't know if she had any erotic feelings, but I fought darn hard to keep mine in check.

We went back to the downtown area of Kyoto; I hailed a taxi which first took Setsuko home and then me to my hotel. Needless to say, I was a very aroused and confused 22 year old. Would Bonnie see this as a kind of cheating on her? Would she understand? And I did write to Bonnie about Setsuko. And what about Setsuko? I got the very distinct impression that her feelings for me were deepening, and the last thing I wanted to do was hurt her.

One day had to be spent shopping. I had a long list and was concerned my money would run out before the list did. Bonnie wanted a set of Noritake china, mother wanted a tea set and dad wanted a bamboo fly rod. Then there were brothers, a sister, a brother-in-law and, last but not least, there were a few items I wanted. I enjoyed the walk from the Rakuyo to down town Kyoto. Since Setsuko worked mornings, I made that walk most every morning. Knowing it would be a full day of shopping I started for town early. The first stop was at a lingerie shop. I wanted to get Bonnie a silk shorty nightgown. I found a small lingerie shop, inside were three clerks, two women and a man. No one could speak English and, of course, I couldn't speak Japanese. It took some doing but finally I conveyed to them what I wanted. One of the female clerks disappeared and returned a short time later with a beautiful floor length gown. I shook my head indicating it wasn't what I wanted. They looked puzzled. I indicated she should hold it up in front of her, which she did. Pointing to my leg, I indicated about mid thigh or shorter. Again they looked puzzled. I don't know how we did it, but at long last they understood that when I got home I was getting married and I wanted a short gown. When they got the message, they looked at each other and, with the women smiling, shook their heads in understanding. At that point the women started talking to each other and then began to giggle. I just smiled. I ended up with a beautiful baby blue silk shorty nightgown. After the purchase was made, they motioned for me to sit down, which I did. One of the women left the room and returned shortly with a bottle of beer and a silk handkerchief; they were gifts. I drank the beer while we conversed largely in sign language, grunts, etc. After I finished the beer, I left amidst bows and thank yous in Japanese. It was a most pleasant experience.

When I reached downtown Kyoto, I started down the thoroughfare and shortly came to a small jewelry store with a small table in front laden with what looked like hand crafted jewelry. I had stopped to admire the pieces when a middle-aged man came out of the store and addressed me in very good English. I asked him about several of the rings he had on the table. He informed me that he had made both the stone and the setting. This intrigued me, and he told me how he made the stone. He then asked me if I had time to sit down and visit for a while. Since the day was set aside for shopping, I welcomed the opportunity. He called to a woman inside and shortly she appeared with two chairs. I thanked her for mine. The gentleman then said something more to her, and soon she appeared with two bottles of beer. This was my second beer and it was relatively early in the morning. He introduced himself as Mr. Keru and the woman as his sister. I thanked her for the beer, and she returned to the inside of the store. Then we commenced our visiting. The first thing Keru wanted to know was what Koreans thought of the Japanese. For almost 50 years,

Korea was occupied by the Japanese military, and they were cruel taskmasters. I told Keru that the Koreans did not like the Japanese. He replied that he understood why and was apologetic for the way the Koreans were treated by the Japanese military. Then he wanted to know about the U.S. He had many questions and I answered them the best I could. A dream of his was to visit the U.S. I hope he was able to realize that dream.

Then it was my turn to ask a few questions. Among other things, I asked him about prostitution in Japan, where at that time, it was legal. I told him it was illegal in the U.S. and that prostitutes had to work clandestinely if they didn't want to run the risk of being arrested by the police. He thought this a rather strange policy, since in Japan prostitution was legal and had a lengthy tradition. "It is common," he told me, "for Japanese businessmen to visit a brothel on their way home after a busy day of work. Prostitutes offer not only sex but also a chance to relax, to visit, and to entertain." I didn't think to ask him what Japanese wives thought of this "cultural nicety." He found the American approach to prostitution as unusual as I found the Japanese. However, his explanation made sense. After all, in Japan, at the time, prostitution was very much a part of the culture milieu. As a result of our discussion, I understood why it was permissible for the prostitutes to enter the outer lobby of the hotel to solicit G.Is.

I don't remember how long we visited, but before I went on my way, I asked him if he would make a ring for Bonnie. He would be most happy to do so. I picked out a setting and a stone, and he told me to return at 3:00 p.m. the next day and the ring would be ready. I left him my class ring since it was very close to Bonnie's size. He then said, "I look forward to your return tomorrow so that we might continue our visit." I returned the next afternoon, but Mr. Keru was not at his place of business. His sister had the ring for me and a note from Keru. In it he had written that business called him away and he regretted very much that we would not be able to continue with our visiting. I paid his sister and then left. I'm sorry I missed Keru. He was a delightful man, well educated, very cosmopolitan and very informative. I hope his desired trip to the U.S. became a reality.

After my visit with Mr. Keru, I went to the Daimaru Department Store, one of Japan's largest department stores. I was after a set of Noritake china for Bonnie. Never before had I seen such a large selection of China. It was difficult choosing a pattern, not knowing exactly what Bonnie had in mind. She wanted something with a floral pattern. A majority of the selections were floral patterns, so I picked a 12 place setting. Since there would be no returning it, she would have to like it. She did. When I paid the bill, I was told that for a nominal fee the store would pack and ship the China to Nebraska. That was a relief since I had no idea how I would go about either packing or shipping so much china. When Bonnie received the two large wooden boxes, not a single dish was broken and not a single piece was either cracked or chipped.

There were various other items to be gotten and, for those I searched out the small shops. It took the better part of the day but at long last my shopping list was exhausted.

Before returning to the hotel, however, I had one bigger item to shop for. Before leaving Clearing Company for Japan, Ju, the Company's barber, asked me if I would buy some velvet for him. When "dressed up," the farm women wore skirts that were made either out of black or purple velvet. I didn't particularly relish the idea of shopping for material for women's dresses, but I couldn't turn Ju down. Of course, I said I would do it. Ju wrote down the order in yards of material. I looked for and found a dry goods store, but I once again had trouble communicating. One female clerk could speak a little English. I told her the order for the material came from a Korean friend. She understood, took the piece of paper with the order written on it and disappeared. After a fairly lengthy time, she returned with the velvet wrapped in two rather large packages. How was I ever going to get it back to Korea? She gave me the bill, and it was right around $200.00. Ju had given me $176.00. I could have covered the $25.00 but I was almost broke and needed every cent I had. I told the clerk the dilemma I was in. Surprisingly, she understood and again disappeared. After a fairly lengthy period of time, she returned and informed me she had spoken with the owner of the store and that she would accept the $176.00 as payment in full under one condition. "Don't tell any of your friends back in Korea that you were able to purchase the material for less than its actual cost." I promised her, and I kept my word though I did tell Ju his estimate of the cost of the material was off by $25.00.

I was tired and though I enjoyed the walk to and from the Rakuyo, I took a taxi back to the hotel. In addition, my arms were full of parcels. This was the only day I spent shopping. I couldn't have done any more even if I had wanted to since my funds were almost depleted. Most of the items were relatively small, and the hotel had made provisions for both packaging and shipping packages. After a shower and a brief rest, I met Setsuko at the restaurant, and we went out for dinner.

The next day was to be my last in Kyoto. One more day and R.&.R. would be over. I dreaded it. I dreaded returning to Korea. I didn't even want to think of this being my last day with Setsuko. My train would be leaving for Kobe about 8:00 p.m. If the past few days were any indication, this day would speed by much too quickly.

At noon I returned to Setsuko's work place. She suggested that instead of going some place we stay at the restaurant. The proprietor had told her she could use one of the private rooms on the second floor, and we could spend the time together there. That suited both of us fine. So we retreated to the seclusion of this very private room. We talked; we just held each other. We reminisced about the week we had spent together, and all that we had done. We avoided any talk about the few hours we had left to be together. Setsuko again asked about Bonnie and our plans. She wanted to know if I would be returning to Kyoto one more time. I told her that I doubted it very much. It was possible that I would earn one more R.&.R. in Japan; however, I now knew that I would not be able to handle another seven days with Setsuko without being unfaithful to Bonnie. I feared I would pressure Setsuko to do something I feel quite sure she perhaps wanted to do but felt constrained not to do. My emotions and sexual dersire were tearing me apart, and I constantly had to remind myself to whom I belonged. In addition, there is no way I would take advantage of Setsuko's kindness toward me. I reasoned that having sex would most likely end up hurting us both, and there was nothing I would do to hurt Setsuko. Oh but the temptation was strong, so very strong. Twenty-two years old and a bundle of unrequited sexual energy. And above all, Bonnie and I had both made vows to be faithful to each other.

Around 5:00 p.m., Setsuko said she had another surprise for me. She was going to serve me supper in the upstairs room. As was the custom, my boots were already off and standing by the door. In the center of the room was a short, squat table, a table that required one to sit in front of cross-legged. Setsuko disappeared and in a short time returned with dinner for two. We ate largely in silence, both of us caught up in our own thoughts. In three hours I would be boarding my train. I wanted the clock to stop but, of course, it didn't. We finished our meal, and then it was time for me to return to the hotel, gather up my few belongings, and head for the depot. Setsuko wanted to come with me. I told her I thought it might be better if she didn't; it might be easier on both of us. However, she insisted and in all honesty, I wanted her to be at the depot when we said our goodbyes. The taxi took us to the Rakuyo Hotel. I gathered up my belongings while Setsuko waited for me in the lobby and then we walked the short distance to the depot. The train would be arriving in a few minutes, so in the interim we made mostly small talk and we were silent for part of the time. And then the train was coming. I turned to Setsuko, who looked up into my eyes with tears running down her cheeks. At that point I could no longer hold back. I put my arms around her, drew her close and kissed her long and hard. When the train stopped, tears were also running down my cheeks. I released her and said one last goodbye and then boarded the train. I stood on the steps as the train moved away from the depot. In a moment Setusuko was out of sight. I sat down and buried my face in my hands. That was the last time

I saw Setsuko, however, she is hardly forgotten. I think of her often and of that week we spent together so many years ago. Is she still living? If she married, which she most likely did, how many children did she have? What did she do with her life? There are times I wish I could find out, however, that is not possible.

Needless to say, the flight back to Seoul was not an enjoyable one, and it was some time before I was able to settle down. I was one confused guy. Had I handled things in the right way? What do I do with my feelings? Thankfully, eventually things returned to normal.

There is a postscript to this chapter. Shortly after returning to Korea, one of my friends went to Kyoto on R.&.R. I wrote a letter to Setsuko; thanking her for the wonderful time she showed me and for her cherished friendship. I told her I cared very much for her and that I would never forget her or the time we spent together. My friend delivered the letter and Setsuko asked him to wait while she wrote me a letter in return. When my friend returned, he gave me the letter, but it was written in Japanese and there was no one to translate it for me. However, I had a hunch what was in it. In 1996 a Japanese woman who worked in the University Bookstore, who had married a G.I, translated the letter. Forty-four years after Setsuko had written the letter, I finally learned of its contents and I had been right. Her feelings for me were very strong. She, like me, was very confused and wondered if there was a future for us. Among other things she wrote, "My comfort comes when I am down and depressed through thoughts of you each day. Though it was short and only a small segment in our lives, our meeting was the most unforgettable event in my life. I only wish you the best. Please take care of yourself as you are heading toward the harsh Korean winter." Although it is yellowed by time, I still have that letter from Setsuko.

In October of 1953, when my friend brought the letter, I decided that I would make no further efforts to contact Setsuko since doing so would do neither of us any good. I hoped that she realized this; I believe she did, for Setsuko was a very intelligent young woman. Above all, I hope she got over me quickly for I would not intentionally have hurt her for the world. Indeed, Setsuko was my little Butterfly, only the outcome was not nearly so tragic.

A TRIP TO THE M.L.R.

For seven months I had been just a couple of miles from the M.L.R., the front line, but never had the opportunity to travel to the area. On a Sunday in October, a truck was dispatched to travel to the M.L.R. Anyone who wanted to tour the battle zones previously held by the 45th Division was invited to make the trip. This was a great opportunity to actually view that area from which so many casualties came to Clearing Company. I had worked a full shift in the E.R., had pulled guard duty, and I was tired. I was determined to make that trip, tired or not.

Since the ceasefire went into effect, the 120th had moved a considerable distance to the east from its old location close to the front line. It would be a long trip over rough, dusty and sometimes dangerous roads, but these were no deterrents. When I traveled in Korea, it was almost always in the back of a truck so the jolting and dust would be nothing new. Since this was the first and only opportunity men from Clearing company had to travel to the former M.L.R., I was surprised at how few opted to make the trip to the area from which so many casualties came. Fortunately, it was not the size of the group that determined whether or not the trip would be made. So long as a few men were interested, the truck was ready to go.

I wanted very much to take color slides of the area and battle sites previously held by the 45th Division so I purchased an ample supply of 35 mm film, the old Kodachrome 10. I was prepared to use it all if necessary. And I did take many slides. The only problem was my camera, the Bolsey B2. Few of the pictures turned out. Most were over exposed even though I used a light meter. After the trip, I concluded that the Bolsey was so much junk and did not use it again to take color slides. Black and white film had more latitude and was much more forgiving.

The few who made up the tour left the Company area at 9:00 a.m. It turned out to be a three hour drive before we got up into the Punch Bowl area. On the way, as we were climbing ever higher, a cock pheasant crossed the road ahead of the truck. I about did a double take. Having been born and raised in south eastern South Dakota in the 1940s and 50s at a time when the pheasant was king, I hunted pheasants every opportunity I had. Believe me, seeing that rooster gave me a real nostalgia trip. A pheasant in Korea? Of course. After all, the full name of the bird is the Chinese Ring Neck Pheasant. South Dakota and all of the States had China to thank for its abundance of pheasants. On several occasions I heard roosters crowing, but this was the only bird I actually saw.

The Punch Bowl was and is a huge clearing nestled down among the mountains. On the very rim of the bowl was what was previously the front line. Only those who were up there could know what it was like. What a hell of a place to have been stationed. The M.L.R. was at the very top of the mountain and overlooked an area that was held by the Chinese. We drove up as close to Sand Bag Castle as we could, and from that vantage point I could see Heartbreak Ridge and Stalin Hill as well as Sand Bag Castle. All three of these battle sites had been pulverized from the constant artillery bombardments. In fact, as far as the eye could see, the ground was churned up and not a living thing could be seen. As a consequence of the Ceasefire, when forces on both sides pulled back 1000 yards, all of these areas fell within the demilitarized zone. Not a thing was moving in no man's land. From our vantage point we could see that most of the sand bag bunkers had been torn down.

Holding the High Ground, Sand Bag Bunkers on the M.L.R.

There were still a few troops occupying different places along the line, however, back of the 1000 yard demilitarized zone. At the time, there were quite a few South Korean troops occupying different places in the area.

From where I stood I could look over into Chinese territory. I saw a large bunker and asked a Lieutenant stationed up there, "What does that house?" He said that it housed about 30 men. Although I glassed it for some time, I saw no movement. The men must have been resting inside. I was surprised to hear the Lieutenant say that the Chinese were still visible from our old positions. I imagined they were keeping their eyes on our troops even as our troops were keeping an eye on them. An artillery outfit on Sandbag Castle had a few high-powered scopes set up, and I was allowed to look through them. This enabled me to get a close up view of the different former battle sites.

An Endless Trench on the M.L.R.

The Lieutenant told me a very interesting story. After the ceasefire went into effect, teams of men from both sides searched the previous battle sites looking for their dead. Some remains were found that had been out there since August of 1950. During the early stages of the war, Heartbreak Ridge was the scene of some very bloody battles. While the search was going on, an American and a Chinese team came together and sat down to visit for a spell. The young Chinese Lieutenant in charge of the search team was a graduate from Yale University. War can encompass some very strange and interesting happening as well as tragic ones.

It turned out to be a very interesting day for me, and in retrospect I wouldn't have missed it for anything. Places that were previously only names, now took on a sense of reality. I came away with some idea, very limited to be sure, of what mountain warfare must have been like. I actually saw a number of well-known battle sites and I saw how the men lived up on the front line and God only knows how they could stand it. I saw Chinese territory and the now peaceful no man's land formed by the 1000 yard pullback. I saw the jagged trenches that stretched for mile upon endless mile. From pictures I had seen, it looked so very much like the battle fields of World War I. As I looked out past the trenches at the churned up, barren ground offering no protection what so ever from the enemy, I couldn't help but think of Stanley Crooks. That is what he crawled out into the night he died.

As I pointed out in the introduction, I am more than a little irritated that there are those in our country who cannot bring themselves to call what transpired in Korea a war, who tend to ignore it when talking about post World War II, the Cold War and the war in Vietnam. How easily we twist language to suit our own personal agendas. Police Action? Conflict? Hell, it was war, a hard war fought under very harsh and difficult conditions. It is just too bad that those who choose to use such terminology couldn't have been up on line when the fighting was going on. If they had been, perhaps they would stop talking about Police Actions, Conflicts, etc. And I am including the generals since most of them die in bed and not on the battlefield.

From time to time I get out those old Kodachrome slides taken with that lousy Bolsey B2 camera. Because most are over exposed, they are not good but they are good enough to remind me what the battlefield in Korea was like once the two sides settled in north of the 38th Parallel.

JUDGE NOT AND BE NOT JUDGED

The Army had done its best to brain wash the troops into believing that the Korean prostitutes were nothing but low life and that all of us would be better off if somehow they could be far removed from the entire Division area. So far as the V.D. rate in the division was concerned, this was, of course, correct. Since so many were mere girls engaging in prostitution to keep alive, the Army didn't have much luck with their efforts to brain wash me against them. As mentioned previously, I have always had a soft spot in my heart for women, and I couldn't bring myself to dislike them and categorize them, as the military would have liked. The process the Army used was much like the one it used on enemy soldiers. They were Gooks they all were Gooks. There never was any attempt to get us to see them as individuals with individual histories, personalities, families, etc. The same approach was used with prostitutes. They were simply prostitutes, not individual girls with unique histories, personalities, and, I would imagine hopes and aspirations. For many, it is likely they had no family.

When on occasion they were brought to Clearing Company, I was generally curious about them. Some were what I would call cute, though heavily made up. Some were out right boisterous and seductive in their speech and in their mannerisms, but mostly they were quiet with down cast eyes. As mentioned above, many were little more than children. Most often when they were brought to Clearing Company, it was for a V.D. check and treatment. Some, however, were brought in suffering extreme abdominal pain often indicative of P.I.D.(pelvic inflamatory disease). How many of these young girls were rendered infecund due to their pelvic infections? "This morning an M.P. brought in another girl caught in the hills last night. Poor kid, what a hell of a life. She was suffering from either a pelvic disorder brought on by V.D. or appendicitis. She was only 21 years old and so small. She had big brown eyes and was a very attractive girl. What kind of a future will she have? The clothes she was wearing were flimsy at best and fit only for summer wear. It turned very cold during the night and I'll bet she and her companions about froze. She had nothing on her feet but a pair of rubber sandals. We transferred her to an ASH where there were female nurses and the necessary equipment to give her a thorough pelvic exam." On occasion, some were brought to Clearing Company in advanced stages of pregnancy. In fact, I was told by an M.P. that one of the girls he picked up was experiencing abdominal discomfort. It was obvious she was pregnant. So instead of bringing her to Clearing company, he took her directly to an ASH, where in a short time she delivered a baby. Why would this girl continue to service the men even though she was many months pregnant? Why would she live under the deplorable conditions, which was the lot of the prostitutes? Why would she put up with the cold and discomfort? The answer is simple: she did so in order to survive. Prostitutes weren't supposed to be treated at an American military medical facility. During the war, this proscription was often over looked. Had they been taken immediately to a Korean medical facility, they most likely would have been given no treatment at all. At Clearing Company they would be given penicillin to treat the pelvic infection or gonorrhea. Yet everyone knew darn well that about as quick as one could say, "prostitute," they would be out plying their trade. And what became of children born to the prostitutes? If they were lucky, they would end up in an orphanage. Christian churches largely ran what orphanages there were. They were full of orphans many being illegitimate children fathered by G.Is. Many were simply left alone to die. If they didn't starve, they froze to death. The 8th Army must have felt some responsibility about this situation, since it launched into an orphanage building program. This was good work for the engineers. In fact, even the 45th Division was building an orphanage on Che Ju Island.

One evening in late October, Jim Mooney and I were on duty in the E.R. At about 7:00, an M.P. in a Jeep drove into the compound with a woman sitting next to him. He came into E.R. and asked us to bring a stretcher since the woman was unable to walk. Jim and I got her onto the stretcher and carried her into the warmth of the E.R. It was then that we noticed that both of her legs, from ankles to mid thigh, were badly burned, third degree burns to be exact. She was in great pain. I asked the M.P. what had happened to her. She had wrapped herself in a blanket and built a fire. Sometime after she had fallen asleep, she turned over and rolled into the fire. Before she was able to extricate herself from the burning blanket, both legs were severely burned. He also informed me that she was a prostitute. He brought her to us so she could be transferred to a Korean medical military unit.

She certainly did not look like the prostitutes we usually saw in E.R. I couldn't help but notice how attractive she was, and the clothing she was wearing was more than a pair of trousers and a blouse fashioned from a G.I. Blanket and G.I. jacket. I estimated her age to be around thirty five.

About this time, Captain Richmond, Clearing Company's Commanding Officer, walked into E.R., took one look at her, and told Jim and I to "Get her out of here fast." The shooting war was now over, and orders from headquarters were unequivocal: do not treat indigenous Korean personnel. If any came into Clearing Company, we were to call an ambulance from a nearby Korean field hospital and tell them we had someone in need of medical treatment and to get over here pronto. So the Captain, being a career military officer, was most reluctant to disobey an order from General Headquarters.

Jim and I pleaded with him to at least let us debride (clean up) the wound. A severe burn like hers should be treated by peeling off the dead skin, by applying a salve like ointment, and then by wrapping the legs with a web-like material that would not adhere to the raw flesh. At first the Captain said, "No." Again we pleaded with him. Finally he said, "All right, go ahead but keep it quiet." We asked him if it would be possible to keep her for the night? He replied, "No way." His reasons were two: l) the General's orders and 2) where would we put a woman in a hospital that held only men? Having said that, he left.

We had our orders. Clean up the burned legs and then see to it she was taken to the Korean field hospital. He also said it would be all right if we used one of our ambulances. He had a tough exterior but inside he was pretty compassionate. After all, he was a doctor.

Poor woman was in severe pain with third degree burns. We could only imagine the extent of the pain. We gave her a shot of morphine and in a very short time the pain subsided. It was then we started a conversation with her. She spoke very good English, and it was obvious she had considerable education. I think both Jim and I kind of fell for her. In addition to being attractive, she was both intelligent and articulate. We asked her how she got burned, and she confirmed what the M.P. had said. She had rolled into a fire she built to keep warm. She then told us she was a prostitute, but she said a lot more. Since she seemed to be in the mood for conversation, I mentioned that she did not fit the image of the prostitutes that we treated at Clearing Company. I then asked her, "Why are you prostituting yourself?" "You G.Is. classify all prostitutes together," she replied. "I like to believe that I am not like the girls that live in the hills. My motives are different," she said. "I am not prostituting myself to keep myself alive but to keep my daughters alive. I have two young daughters who are living with a family in Pusan and so long as I keep sending money, the family has agreed to take care of them. Should the money stop coming, my daughters will be put out on the street." Although she told us the age of her daughters, I do not recall what they were. She also told us that her husband was dead, killed when the North invaded Seoul. Before the invasion, they would have been classified as a well established middle class family. She had no other family that could take over the support of her daughters. She was most concerned that her injuries would prevent her from continuing in her work as a prostitute. Almost in a state of panic and certainly aware of the seriousness of her condition she said, "If I can't work, what is going to happen to my daughters?" Poor woman, there was nothing we could say to comfort her.

As we conversed with her, we picked off the dead skin. The third degree burns were complete; there wasn't a cubic centimeter of leg or thigh that was covered with unburned skin. After we had pulled off the dead skin we washed her legs with a solution that would cleanse but not burn; I believe it was called physoderm. Of course, everything we did was only temporary. Upon reaching the Korean field hospital, she would need more intensive care. We had done all that we could. The danger was that if she didn't receive that care in short order she would develop gangrene. This malady, at the very least, would necessitate amputation of her legs and possibly cost her her life.

Finally, at about 11:00, we were finished. Mindful of Captain Richmond's order, Chico (Beltram Carmello, who was also on duty) volunteered to accompany the ambulance driver to the Korean field hospital. We informed him what to tell the Korean doctor and to remind him that haste was of the utmost importance. We gave her one last pain killing injection, wrapped a blanket around her, and reluctantly placed her in the back of the ambulance.

When the ambulance returned and Chico came into E.R., we could tell that his conversation with the Korean doctor had not gone well. Regardless of the reasons for doing so, Koreans had little use for their prostitutes. Chico explained to the Korean doctor that she was in need of immediate attention lest gangrene set in. The doctor told him that he had more important cases to work on. He ordered her placed in an unheated tent where she would stay for at least two days before he would be able to work on her injuries. Two days were sufficient for gangrene to develop. Although we had no way of finding out, most likely she died. With her death, the care of her daughters probably came to an end. What happened to them? Had it not been for the stupid order from the General, we could have evacuated her to the 121st Evacuation Hospital in Seoul or at least to an ASH, where she could have gotten the care she so desperately needed.

At the same time, it is possible that the order sent down from the General originated from much higher up the chain of command and that no 8th Army medical facility would have accepted and treated her.

She taught me something about making judgments before the facts were received. It's so easy to be critical. How many women would not prostitute themselves if that was the only way to keep their children alive? The memory of her bothers me, even today. In more optimistic moments, I want to believe she received the treatment she needed and survived.

"MERRY CHISTMAS FROM KOREA, 1953: THE ARMY REGRETS TO INFORM YOU THAT YOUR SON..."

The spirit of Christmas was in the air. Not a culture with a religion other than Christianity, not 10,000 miles separating me from home, not a current environment that was doing nothing to extol the virtues of Christmas, none of these could dull the excitement and the euphoria of the coming season. Helping it along, of course, were letters from home telling of preparations going on back there, and letters in which the expressions of love seemed more enhanced. Christmas 1952 was quite different. That one had a touch of apprehension, a bit of sadness, an aching heart knowing the girl I loved would be unavailable to me for at least the next 12 months and maybe more. As it turned out, quite a bit more. But this Christmas, the season held promise. It would be the last in Korea; the war was at a stalemate. That is all a ceasefire really is, a stalemate. Although the shooting could break out again any day, that scenario didn't appear very likely. So the worst that could happen was another six months of harassment, another six months of reminders that my buddies and I were men in skirts

There were at Clearing Conmpany, 120th Medical Battalion, a number of young Korean soldiers, KATUSA, (Korean Augmentation to the United States Army) who were with us on temporary duty. They viewed all of this Christmas anticipation with a bit of bewilderment. Since most did not speak English, it was difficult to convey to them the reason for the Christmas spirit that was so apparent.

135

Our Katusa Boys

One day in early December, I took two of the young men, boys really, with me, and we went into the mountains looking for a small pine tree that would suffice for a Christmas tree. I should point out that the mountains, at least the mountains in South Korea, were devoid of trees, having been cut down perhaps centuries earlier for firewood. Instead the mountains were covered with shrubs and brush. Every now and then, however, I would see a small pine tree and was hoping there just might be one near the compound. I can't recall how long we looked but lo and behold, we found a little tree about two and one half to three feet tall. I cut it down and we carried it back to our squad tent. I got a saw, hammer, a few nails and a few pieces of wood from the supply tent and built a stand for the little tree. And then we decorated that little tree. By we, I mean all of my tent mates and even the Korean boys. Our decorations were very primitive, but they did give the tent a holiday look. Primarily we used aluminum foil and white photo flash bulbs, the small kind. We fashioned a star out of cardboard, covered it with aluminum foil, and attached it to the top of the tree. It wasn't much, but it added to the Christmas spirit.

All of us in the tent had received packages from home. In fact, In November I had received a Christmas present of sorts from the Army. I was promoted to sergeant. From private to sergeant in 14 months wasn't bad. Christmas had no meaning to the Korean boys; however, we felt we couldn't be opening our packages while there was nothing for them. We all chipped in a few dollars and delegated two fellows to go to the P.X. to do some Christmas shopping for the Korean boys. The items weren't much, shaving lotion, toothbrush and toothpaste, razors, etc. Actually, there wasn't much more in the P.X. than cosmetics. Nonetheless, for the boys who made an equivalent of about thirty-six cents a month, the gifts were considerable and their eyes shone with excitement as they opened their packages. Just watching them made us feel good inside.

On December 15th, just 10 days before Christmas, I was in the E.R., most likely trying to keep warm. I don't believe I was pulling night duty at this time. My Raynaud's disease was flaring up and the heat in the squad tent was far from adequate. It was okay if the troops froze, but the patients had to have ample heat. As a result, even when not on duty, I spent a lot of time in the E.R. The winters in Korea are much like the winters in the Dakotas and Montana. Snow is frequent and temperatures can plunge to as low as 20 degrees below zero. There was literally nothing but canvas between the elements and us. Each tent had two squat, round stoves, but we never were allowed to turn them up to where they would warm the tent if even a little. During the nighttime, stoves had to be turned so low that the fire burned only several inches out from the oil outlet. Actually only a small finger of flame flickered. Guards were supposed to check to see to it that no stoves were turned higher than one or two on a dial that reached to ten. If they found any stoves higher than two, they had orders to turn off the stove completely. The fact that the temperature might have been below zero made no difference. I would pile on all the clothing I could, including my parka with fur lined hood, several pairs of socks, etc., and then crawl into my sleeping bag and immediately assume a fetal position. As long as I didn't move, I could keep relatively warm, however, just a slight change of position and instantly I would be freezing. The heat of the E.R. was welcome, and that is where I spent much time.

And so it was that I happened to be in the E.R.on the evening of December 15. It was around 7:00 p.m. when one of the fellows from a regimental aid station pulled up driving an ambulance. He walked into the E.R. and looking around saw me. "Hey Sergeant Waltner," he said, "I've got four fellows in the ambulance on sick call. Would you mind getting information on them and bringing them into the E.R.?" I wasn't on duty, but I grabbed a clipboard and the forms necessary to get name, rank, serial number, outfit and nature of physical complaint. When I stepped outside, I noticed that there were no voices emanating from the ambulance. This is rare since as a rule the fellows would be visiting and joking around. I walked around to the back of the ambulance and opened the doors. Immediately I knew something was wrong. There were four fellows in the ambulance all right; all were lying on their backs on the bunks that lined the sides of the ambulance. I stepped inside and said, "Hi fellows, what seems to be the trouble?" No one moved. All remained silent. Then the realization hit me: they were all dead. It took a lot to shake me up, but this time I was shook up good. This was December 15. The shooting war had ended almost five months earlier, yet here were four men dead from what appeared to be shrapnel wounds. I had heard nothing that the shooting war had started up again, but these men were battle casualties. I sat down on the very edge of one of the bunks and just stared at the men. Death is so silent, so unmoving. I had to get their names off their dog tags so I got up and bent over each fellow and lifted the dog tag on the chain around his neck. And then I noticed something I had not seen before on a dead body. All of them had what appeared to be goose bumps on their dead flesh. I thought this so unusual that the sight of those goose bumps stuck in my mind. After I took down their names and serial numbers, I again sat down on the edge of one of the bunks. If I could have, I would have wept. After awhile I left the ambulance and walked back into the E.R. and asked the driver what had happened to the four men. What happened was that the regiment was holding an exercise and using live ammunition and artillery rounds. Eight men were in a make shift fox hole under the long stump of a tree when an incoming artillery round fell short, hit the tree, exploded and showered fragments down upon the unsuspecting men. The four in the ambulance were killed outright while the other four were all critically wounded. Since I had the information needed for a report to the Division Headquarters and since they had already been pronounced dead, the ambulance driver took the bodies on down the road to graves registration.

After he left, I sat in the E.R. in a very somber and pensive mood. Back home were four sets of parents, wives maybe, children, brothers and sisters, whose anxiety and concern surely lessened considerably when the cease-fire went into effect. At least they would no longer need to worry about their loved ones being killed in action. In addition, this being the 15th of December, they most likely had already made up Christmas packages filled with items their sons, husbands, etc., could use and filled with the kind of love that only the Christmas season can engender. Now they were about to get a totally unexpected Christmas message. Who could have told them that whereas they no longer had to worry about their loved ones dying from enemy fire, there always had to be some concern that they would be killed by "friendly fire." Friendly fire? What in the world is that when it can kill you? Even though it would be several decades before the concept came into being and usage, that is an oxymoron if ever there was one. As I sat there, I could envision the men's family members maybe offering up a prayer of thanksgiving that their son was no longer in danger. This was the 15th; it would be just about Christmas Eve or Christmas Day when they received that much-dreaded message. "Merry Christmas from Korea, 1953: Dear Parent, wife, etc., the Army regrets to inform you that your son…" God in Heaven, what a Christmas present. Parents weep for your sons; wives weep for your husbands for there will be no weeping over here. It was a time when weeping seemed to be the only appropriate response.

MARILYN

Yes, The Marilyn, Marilyn Monroe. Rumor had been circulating for some time that Marilyn Monroe was going to give a show at the 120th amphitheater, Thunderbird Bowl. Now when a show like this was brought to the amphitheater, any G.I. within the Division who was not on duty could attend. Throughout the Division, transportation was provided. Thunderbird Bowl was spruced up. Much sand was moved from one spot to another and then back again. Whenever anything "important" took place at the Bowl, sand always had to be moved. If it hadn't been for moving sand, I don't think the work detail would have had anything to do. I must admit, however, that Thunderbird Bowl looked real spiffy for Marilyn appearance.

The officers were in a high state of excitement as the day of Marilyn's arrival neared. I can't recall much excitement on the part of the enlisted men at Clearing Company,120th Medical Battalion. We had long ago learned that when females arrived at 120th, enlisted men were to keep out of the way.

February 20th, 1954, finally arrived. Marilyn was supposed to make a grand entry by helicopter at 3:00 p.m. Thunderbird Bowl was packed with men from nearly every unit in the Division. There was standing room only. By this time each unit's P.X. was overflowing with goods from Japan. As a consequence almost everyone had a camera and everyone wanted a picture or pictures of Marilyn. Three-thirty rolled around. No Marilyn. Three-forty-five rolled around and still no Marilyn. This was February and darkness set in quite early. Finally, just as the sun was about to slip behind the mountains, Marilyn's helicopter arrived. When she stepped out on the stage, there was a stampede of human bodies surging forward as everyone wanted to get that picture of Marilyn in the flesh before it got dark. Several men were knocked to the ground and trampled, suffering various injuries, injuries that had to be treated in the E.R.

In my humble opinion, I felt that Marilyn Monroe was rather disappointing. She was a very attractive young woman and good to look at to be sure, but I didn't think she could act or sing. And young she was. In 1954 Marilyn would have been 28 years old. In all fairness to Marilyn, it must have been down right hard to put on a solo performance and to sing with a band that could barely make harmonic music.

I never saw so many officers on the stage of Thunderbird Bowl. They crowded around her almost hiding her from the view of the enlisted men seated on the benches and standing around the periphery. They reminded me of a bunch of male dogs crowding in on a bitch in heat.

Marilyn was to spend the night at 120th. The following morning she wanted to go through the wards to do what she could to "cheer up" the men. I can't recall where she slept but undoubtedly we had a V.I.P. tent. After all, we always seemed able to put U.S.O. personnel up for the night.

Shortly before Marilyn's arrival, a number of photographic slides of her in the nude were circulating at Clearing Company. Some of these pictures still surface from time to time today. One slide in particular has Marilyn, nude as a jaybird, stretched out on a bed, complete with a velvet bedspread. One of our officers was especially enamored of Marilyn, so his fellow officers decided to have some fun with him. Unknown to him, they rigged up a 35 mm slide projector in his tent with the lens aimed at his cot. The projector was rigged to turn on when the officer pulled the string to his overhead light bulb. He came into his tent, pulled the string and for a moment got a thrill of a lifetime or so his buddies assumed. Wouldn't have surprised me one bit if, for a moment, he actually believed Marilyn was lying on his bed. Of course, his buddies got a big charge out of his imagined reaction.

The next morning Marilyn went through the wards. Of course, there weren't any battle casualties, and I don't know what she expected to find.

As she went from cot to cot and greeted the fellows, she would remark, "You don't look very sick to me." A real morale booster for the fellows, to be sure. At the same time, just being so close to Marilyn most likely made them completely oblivious to what she said.

Shortly after, Marilyn left Clearing Company, and it was surprising how quickly things returned to normal. I am sure for many men it was a thrill of a lifetime to see Marilyn in the flesh. However, having always preferred brunettes, Blondes were just not my forte. Although she was a pretty young woman I can't say that Marilyn caused my pulse to quicken

From that point forward, Marilyn's life seemed to have been a succession of unhappy events. Given the notoriety that followed her over the next few years, I am glad I had the opportunity to see her and to hear her in the flesh. Marilyn died in 1962 from an apparent overdose of sleeping pills. She was only 36 years old.

A Broken Promise

With the deepening of fall and the stupidity of not allowing the stoves to be turned on, I was beginning to have trouble with my hands and feet. They were always cold, no matter how heavy my socks or how many pairs of gloves I wore. Although I was becoming increasingly uncomfortable, I didn't give it too much thought, assuming that once we had heat in the tent the problem would resolve itself. Not so. One evening I took off my boots, and my feet had a blackish gray color. In addition, my left arm and hand also had a dark appearance. Now I was concerned about frostbite. A short time later I developed blisters on both my hands and feet. These were extremely painful.

I was now sufficiently alarmed that I placed myself on sick call. All three doctors, including Captain Richmond, thoroughly examined my hands and feet. The three doctors went into a huddle and, when they finished their deliberations, told me that I had Raynaud's disease or phenomenon. Raynaud's disease is a peripheral vascular disorder, which in my case was brought on by cold weather injury. Because of the continuous cold that my feet and hands were subject to, the surface blood vessels or capillaries in the areas that had been affected were damaged permanently. The result was that cold temperatures caused the capillaries and blood vessels to constrict thus restricting an adequate flow of blood to my extremities. As a consequence I was at extreme risk of losing fingers and toes and possibly hands and feet.

After giving me this discouraging report, Dr. Richmond said, "Sergeant Waltner, by rights we should evacuate you to Japan where you will be able to work in an environment that is constantly warm. You are needed here so I have ruled out evacuation. Instead, you are hereby ordered to wear your heavy winter clothing at all times, especially your thermo boots. Should I catch you without them, it will be a court marshal offense." A court marshal offense when I should have been evacuated? That sounded plain crazy. I would have liked to believe that the good doctor would not have me court marshaled had I stepped outdoors with leather boots. I really didn't know if Captain Richmond would follow through on his threat or not. I had never manifested any of these symptoms while living in South Dakota with a climate equally severe. As a youth I was often outside hunting or trapping during the winter months without experiencing any problems, so it was obvious that my Raynaud's disease was service connected.

Captain Richmond gave me one more piece of advice: "When you get back to the states and during the process of being discharged, be sure you file for compensation since the condition is likely to worsen as you get older." And, of course, it has to the point that when exposed to even slight cold, my hands turn numb; and the only way to restore the blood flow is to immerse them in very warm water.

I was speechless. I had a potentially crippling disease and should have been evacuated to Japan. However, I was needed at Clearing Company so I would not be evacuated. And to think that I always thought in the military no one was indispensable. Over the months, hundreds of men were evacuated, but when I had cause to be, the powers that be would not evacuate me. Unbelievable.

As the cold progressed, my feet and hands gave me more and more trouble and the symptoms of Raynaud's got worse. I would take off my thermo boots, and my feet would be discolored with blister like lesions forming on them. Blisters also developed on my fingers. Of course, both feet and hands were constantly cold; there was just no way of warming them.

I found it necessary to talk to Dr. Richmond again. He didn't like what he saw and admitted I was at risk of severe cold weather injury, but he was not ready to transfer me to Japan and a warmer clime. He reminded me that I was badly needed and that they (the doctors) would do their best to control the Raynaud's with limited time outdoors, with proper clothing and foot wear, and with priscoline, a vasodilator, a drug that was supposed to open the peripheral blood vessels. I guess I was fortunate I didn't lose toes or fingers. Had I ever been caught outdoors over night, there is no question that I would have lost appendages. Being caught outdoors during the winter months for an extended period is a fear I carry with me today. It is always possible that having an automobile breakdown or getting lost while hunting, etc., could occur. As a rule, during the fall, winter, and spring months, I am over dressed, never under dressed.

When I transferred to the Medical Clearing Company, 2nd Infantry Division in February 1954, Captain Richmond gave me a letter in which he advised the Commanding Officer that I be given special consideration in assigning me, an assignment that excluded duty outdoors. The logical time to transfer me to Seoul or Japan would have been during the phase out of the 45th Division, including Clearing Company, 120th Medical Battalion. By his own admission, Richmond had every reason to do so, but he steadfastly refused to send me out of Korea. I wondered at the time and many times since what his real reason was.

It was either in late 1953 or early 1954 that President Eisenhower promised that just as soon as possible two divisions would be rotated back to the U.S. First, it was a rumor that the 45th Division would be one of those divisions and then it was a reality. The other Division was the 40th. I was elated since I assumed that the rotation of a division meant just that. How wrong I was. Only the men eligible for rotation in February and March would accompany the Division home. It was to be little more than a return of the colors of the Division to the States. Rotation was set for sometime between February 15th and March 15th. Those of us not eligible for rotation would be transferred to an 8th Army unit or to one of the divisions remaining in Korea. Although I should have known better, I thought that my Raynaud's disease would qualify me to return to the States with the Division. My naivete' was increasing.

As men from Clearing Company, 120th Medical Battalion, were being sent to various medical units through South Korea, I was reassigned to the Medical Clearing Company, 2nd Infantry Division. This seemed rather odd to me. Following the decision to rotate the 45th Division to the States, Dr. Kretzchmar had assured me that, contrary to what Captain Richmond had been saying, he would now see to it that I would be transferred either to Seoul or to Japan. Apparently he was more concerned about my condition than was Captain Richmond. However, something just wasn't right. I couldn't be going to Seoul or Japan and the 2nd Infantry Division at the same time. Dr. Kretzchmar's rational for evacuating me to Seoul or Japan was his fear that I would end up as a line medic at the 2nd Division. If that happened, I would lose both toes and fingers. In fact, on the 22nd of February, he signed an E.M.T. (Emergency Medical Transfer tag). That was very timely for I had lost all feeling in one of my fingers, and fairly lengthy heat therapy to restore feeling was required This was the basis of his concern. His words were to the effect that after I closed my records and books and turned them into Division Headquarters, I would hop a plane at the 629th Clearing Company and fly to the 121st Evacuation hospital in Seoul for further disposition. So here it was, finally the assurance that I would at long last be going somewhere where I would be warm. Or so I thought, but I still had doubts since this came from Kretzchmar and not Richmond. There is no question that Dr. Kretzchmar had taken a genuine interest in my case. One evening he told me, "Sergeant Waltner, be assured that you will not be going to the 2nd Infantry Division as assigned, but to Seoul and perhaps from there to Japan." In spite of Kretzchmar's assurance, it didn't happen.

How could Dr. Kretzchmar promise me I would be evacuated to the 121st Evacuation Hospital and Dr. Richmond so casually ignore the promise? Easy. Dr. Kretzchmar was a draftee; he would put in his time and return to his private practice. As a rather interesting aside, after Kretzchmar had finished his time in the Army, I learned that he joined the teaching faculty at the University of Michigan Medical School at Ann

Arbor. Some years later, a very good friend of mine enrolled in the Medical School at the University of Michigan. He had Dr. Kretzchmar as a teacher. He didn't give a darn about the Army and its rules. He saw himself as my doctor and me as his patient and on the basis of my condition he made what he believed to be the only reasonable decision.

Captain Richmond was a career man, an organization man. It was obvious that to him the needs of the organization came first. This was reflected in his stubborn refusal to evacuate me. He lacked the sympathetic concern shown by Bill Kretzchmar. Further, he would be going in one direction and I in another. And once both of us left the compound, in his mind Waltner would cease to exist. It was very easy for him to countermand Dr. Kretzchmar's orders. Even if Kretzchmar had still been around, I believe Richmond would have done exactly what he did. In addition, Kretzchmar was a Lieutenant and Richmond was a Captain. In the military, that makes all the difference in the world.

And so those plans, so carefully crafted by Dr. Kretzchmar, were abruptly cancelled by Captain Richmond. Dr. Kretzchmar had left the area, rotating to some other hospital. Dr. Richmond was still around. He and I would be among the last men to leave Clearing Company, 120th Medical Battalion. On the 26th of February, I finished with all medical records and books. While filling out my evacuation card, Captain Richmond came into what was left of the E.R. He called S-1 to see how my evacuation plans would impact the plans to transfer me to the 2nd Division. He was told that there would be too much red tape involved. He agreed fully with S-1, and with his agreement, any chance I had of being evacuated to Seoul or Japan evaporated. I was sure that Kretzchmar had Richmond's concurrence on his decision to transfer me because Richmond was his superior officer and commanding officer. Kretzchmar, however, was gone and he never would find out if my evacuation took place. Richmond knew that. I had believed the promise and it evaporated in a moment, in the twinkling of an eye. Funny thing is, I really believed the Captain was a friend. How naive I was. I should have known there is a difference between being friendly and being a friend. It was my mistake to confuse the two. I would stay in Korea and with the 2nd infantry Division until time to rotate home. Disappointed, sure. It was a bitter pill to swallow. Just being in the military meant disappointment. Now that my work was finished, I had nothing to do but wait for orders to ship out for the 2nd Division.

Goodbye 45th Division, Hello 2nd Division

Almost immediately upon receiving word that the 45th Division would be one of two divisions to rotate back to the States, the process began. The transitional month would be February. Between February 15th and March 15th, all units within the Division would be closing down; Clearing Company, 120th Medical Battalion was no exception. After just one year in the 45th Division, upon reassignment I would be leaving for one of the five divisions remaining in Korea. At the time I had no idea which division it would be. As it turned out it was to be the 2nd Division. I would be leaving the area that had come to be home for seven long months. I would bid goodbye to some very close friends, men that I had gone through basic training with and been with for the many months already spent in Korea. We had been together for 17 months.

As February progressed, the number of men showing up on sick call grew increasingly smaller. Unless they were really sick, most had important things to attend to such as getting ready for the coming transfer. Before all medical records were turned in, however, the number on sick call again picked up for a time. The decision was made that Clearing Company, 120th Medical Battalion would become Clearing Company, 24th Infantry Division. In effect, the whole unit would be transferred over to the 24th Division. One consequence was that as the men from the 24th Division began to arrive, the number reporting in on sick call increased.

Early in the month I was called to the Control Post to state my choice of unit to which I desired to be transferred. I said I would like to go to an 8th Army medical unit. I really don't know why the Division went

149

through this malarkey since we, all of us at Clearing Company, would be sent to where the powers that be wanted to send us. I did not end up at an 8th Army medical unit.

On February 7th word came down that the 120th Medical Battalion hospital units would close on the 14th, at which time I would be relieved of all duties. Then on the 3rd of March the Division would be leaving for home. As was so typical of the Army, the schedule did not turn out that way. I stayed at the hospital until the 28th of February, and it wasn't until about the 15th of March that the Division finally sailed for home. As indicated earlier, the move was largely ceremonial and a move on paper. Most of the Division's armament and equipment would be transferred to a ROK unit or units. No big guns, no tanks, none of that would return with the Division. Only the men eligible to rotate in February and March would be going home with the Division. Home for the 45th Infantry Division was Oklahoma, since it was an Oklahoma National Guard Division.

"I went down to the 45th Division Rotation Parade today. You should have seen all the generals. I must have counted up to 20 of them. It was a mighty impressive parade. It's impossible to imagine the might of a division, such as the 45th. It can only be witnessed and it is tremendous. The parade was also quite colorful with various floats. Rockets were constantly being fired into the air. I even got to see Korean President, Sigman Rhee, who was at the parade as a guest of honor."

Of course, there had to be a rotation parade for the 45th Division and what a parade it was. All units of the Division were involved. Such a show of immense firepower was most impressive. Passing by in review were tanks, big guns, thousands of troops, various floats etc. All that power of one division and the 45th was only one of seven or eight divisions in Korea, and all we could do was fight a holding action for almost three years. Incredible.

The men of the 120th Clearing Company were now leaving in sizable groups, 30 or 40 at a time. The Company was rapidly losing its manpower. Of course, large numbers of men were no longer needed since, as our troops pulled out, the troops from the 24th Division replaced them. In fact, there was so little to do that one morning Captain Richmond declared an unofficial holiday. I do believe he did this on his own, the order or permission did not come down from the General at Division Headquarters.

On the 17th of February the men rotating back to the States with the 45th Division, left for the rendezvous point. It would be a couple of weeks before they would board a ship for the return trip home. With their leaving, a colorful page in the history of the 45th Division would come to an end.

On the 19th of February I saw the transfer list. My name was on it and, as I had been told, I would be going to the 2nd Infantry Division, the Indian Head Division. It is worthy of comment that the 2nd Division was the only division to remain in Korea and remains there to this day.

"For the first time since basic training, I awoke at 5:30 on the morning of the 23rd to the sound of reveille being played on a bugle instead of on a record blaring over the P.A. system. I about flew out of my sleeping bag. It was played for the benefit of some of the men that were leaving the Company for their new assignments. I wanted to see them off so I got dressed and went outside to bid them goodbye. I've been with most of these guys since I arrived in Korea, just short of a year ago. On Thursday and Saturday a.m., more will be leaving. This is a depressing time for me seeing so many of my friends leave and knowing I will not see them again"

"Today (February 26th) I was quite pleasantly surprised. I was working on my final reports when about 9:30 the First Sergeant called and told me to report to the C.P. with full dress uniform, polished combat boots and purple scarf. I hurried down to the C.P. as quickly as I could. From the C.P. I went down to Battalion S-1, where in a brief ceremony I was presented with the Bronze Star, a citation and medal for meritorious service. Believe me, I was quite taken aback. To me, at least, it was quite an honor to receive that decoration. Believe me when I say that receiving such an award was the least of my expectations." I looked so sharp all dressed up in my best uniform that I should have grabbed a Moose-a-Maid (Korean girl), stole a jeep, drove into Seoul and did up the town. Instead I went back to the tent, changed into my fatigues and continued to wait for the transfer to the 2nd Division.

On the evening of the 27th, Ken Worthington, Company Clerk and long time friend and the only other soldier from Clearing Company to be reassigned to the 2nd Division, came to the tent and told the remaining Thunderbirds to report to the N.C.O. (Non Commissioned Officers) Club pronto. When I walked in, there were Captain Richmond and Lt. Neveaux standing behind the bar. Lined up on the bar were five fifths of whiskey. Captain Richmond announced that no one was to leave the club until all five bottles had been disposed of. So, we set to it. The cook made some sandwiches; we popped some corn and had a high old time. The party broke up at 11:30 and, yes, the five bottles of whiskey were empty. I was feeling a little high but all things considered, not bad. What really surprised me was that both Captain Richmond and Lt. Neveaux took off their rank insignia for the occasion, and for once, just once, they were regular guys. Lt. Neveaux and I had become good friends. He was about my age, perhaps a year or two older, and hailed from Minnesota. At 120th Clearing Company, I believe he had served as Supply Officer. He was transferred to an outfit located just a few miles from the 2nd Division Clearing Company, and we would get together a time or two before he rotated home.

My last letter to Bonnie from Clearing Company, 120th Medical Battalion, was written on the morning of February 28th. "Tomorrow a.m., at 7:00, I will leave for Ch,unch,on and Division Rear. I should leave Division Rear for the 2nd Division on Tuesday. My new address will be, Clearing Company, 2nd Medical Battalion, 2nd Infantry Division, A.P.0. 248, C/O P.M., San Francisco, California."

On March 1, Ken Worthington and I hopped into the back of a truck and left the Company area for Division Rear. With our leaving, only six fellows from Clearing Company would be left in the area, and they would be leaving for Headquarters Company the next morning at 8:00. On March 2nd, Ken and I would be with the 2nd Infantry Division. Goodbye 45th Infantry Division.

By 7:00 a.m. on March 2nd Ken and I boarded one of those slow moving trains at Ch'unch'on on our way to 2nd Division Rear. Although it was a cold trip since the cars were not heated, the sun coming through the windows provided some solar radiation. I found the trip to be a most interesting one. The slow ride gave me a chance to see yet another part of Korea. Although the countryside was similar to Yangu Valley, home of the 120th, I noticed that there were more farms as we gradually rode east. The areas the farmers could occupy had slowly been increasing, although a boundary line existed beyond which they could not go. It was still much too early to be working in the rice paddies; however, I could see the neat pattern they made. No land was wasted, with some of the paddies going right up the sides of the hills.

I also had a chance to see a number of Korean villages. Up to this point, Ch'unch'on was the only village I had any familiarity with and, because of the devastation that had taken place there, it was largely a cardboard village. Most of the villages looked the same. The houses were built on a wooden frame, paper, glass and thatched siding and roof. There were no sidewalks and no curbs and gutters. Sometimes paths served as dirt roads. I was impressed with the large number of children on their way to school. Typical to a traditional society, Korean couples had numerous children. The larger the family, the more land that could be worked. The larger the family, the greater assurance the couple had that they would be taken care of in their old age.

The ride to 2nd Division Rear took about three and one-half hours. It is to be remembered that from west to east South Korea is only about 100 miles wide. We were getting close to the Ch'orwon Valley area, the area the North Korean Army swept through on its way south and the area in which a number of famous battle sites (Old Baldy, etc.) were located. These places saw intense fighting back in July of 1953. Actually, the fighting was intense

along the entire length of the front line, from west to east. What I hadn't
realized when reassigned to the 2nd Division was that the 2nd was still on
line. A number of American Divisions had been replaced on line with
ROK Divisions. The American Divisions were in reserve in rear areas fully
ready to return to the front should fighting break out once again. We were
still in North Korea and the countryside was still mountainous, although
gradually I was seeing more and more level areas

At 11:00 a.m. we reached 2nd Division Rear. Ken and I were issued the
Indian Head Patch, the official patch of the 2nd Division and, so far as I
was concerned, the most attractive patch in all of Korea. Since there was
no longer a 45th Division presence in Korea, it was appropriate for us to
remove the 45th Thunderbird patch from our right shoulder and replace
it with the Indian Head patch of the 2nd Division. The Thunderbird
patch was shifted to our left shoulder where it rightfully belonged. This we
did as soon as time permitted.

Since we had already been assigned to the 2nd Division, on paper at
least, there wasn't much processing to be done. In addition, we were
already carrying our full complement of winter clothing with us. We were
told, however, that on the morrow we would be given a lengthy talk on
the history of the 2nd Division by an old Master Sergeant who had been
in the Army 36 years and in the 2nd Division for almost that long. The
old Sarge was from North Dakota. Why, in the states, we were literally
next-door neighbors. And we did get that talk. It was both lengthy and
interesting. The Sergeant covered not only the history of the Division during World War II, but also its battles in Korea from the day of its arrival.

Having been assigned to the Clearing Company, 2nd Medical
Battalion,we rode the short distance to our new home that afternoon.
Home it would be until our rotation back to the States.

The 2nd Division Clearing Company was structured much as was the
45th Division Clearing Company. There were an E.R., three hospital
wards and a neuropsychiatry ward. Before leaving the 45th, I had heard

that the 2nd Division was not quite as steeped in "Mickey Mouse" as was the 45th. As it turned out, however, that was not the case.

In many ways the 2nd Division was still on a war footing. We had total blackouts starting at 9:00 p.m. In addition, there were alerts several times a week. A siren would blow and I would grab my steel pot (helmet) and run up a mountainside where a number of bunkers and foxholes were located. I was not allowed to forget for a moment that what was signed at Panmunjon was only a cease-fire and not an armistice. The shooting could break out at any moment, and the Division was taking no chances. Sometime the alerts came during the daylight hours and sometimes at night. And since the 2nd was up on line, there was no loitering on the way to the relative safety of the bunkers and foxholes.

Reveille was held every morning at 6:45, followed by breakfast and then a police call at 8:00 a.m. In addition, there was a half hour of calisthenics every day, which suited me fine. I had discovered with the first alert, when I had to run up the mountainside, that I was badly out of shape. Each Wednesday evening there was a Battalion retreat for the N.C.Os. at which general items were discussed and explained. From time to time, there was also a T.I.&E. (Troop Information and Education) class held in the afternoon.

Spring was just around the corner, and we were no longer experiencing the extreme cold of January and February. I was still wearing thermo boots, however. Made of rubber, they did not "breathe" as leather did, and as a result, my feet were always wet and clammy. With Captain Richmond no longer around to monitor my attire, I put on my leather boots to see if I could get by without experiencing damage to my feet. The leather boots worked out just fine.

Whereas Clearing Company, 120th Medical Battalion served men only from the Division as well as attached Korean personnel and any foreign contingents attached to the Division (we had a Phillipino and Dutch Battalions attached), 2nd Division Clearing Company served many 8th Army units as well as 2nd Division personnel and a Thai Battalion. As a result, sick call was usually very large, 100 men or more per day. Many of those showing up on sick call were coming for a return visit. Often it would be mid-afternoon before all patients had been seen. The doctors, however, kept their cool and checked returnees as if each visit had been their first visit. Some men were gold bricking, but some were suffering from psychosomatic ills brought on by the tedium, boredom and nonsense of the Army. And, of course, everyone wanted to go home. Routine were circumcisions, hemorrhoidectomies, removal of warts, etc, all under local anesthetics. Instead of referring a patient to an ASH unit as we so frequently did at the 45th before the cease-fire, the doctors instead sent most referrals on to a nearby MASH unit.

Many men were coming in requesting circumcision even though the physical need for such was not indicted for most. Some were experiencing phimosis and for them surgery was a real blessing. I came to the conclusion for many circumcission was for cosmetic purposes. Most men had been circumcised as infants and some men who were uncircumcised felt awfully conspicuous. After it had been performed, there was more than one man who wished he had not had the operation. A circumcision for a baby is one thing, but for an adult male, it can be quite an ordeal. In addition I saw some botched jobs that made the men wish they had left well enough alone. Unfortunately for them, once removed there was no reattaching a severed foreskin. One patient I remember in particular. The circumcision was routine, and after a couple of days the man was sent back to his unit. This was in the morning. About 3:00 p.m. a buddy brought him to the E.R. The poor guy was in absolute agony. In fact, he was shaking from the pain. Apparently he had experienced an erection, and who ever did the operation must have done a poor job of suturing the skin of the shaft to the flap of skin left intact just behind the frenulum. All of the stitches had pulled out. When he came into the E.R., no doctor was present and one had to be rounded up. Like the enlisted men, after duty hours the doctors would also engage in sports activities such as softball, volleyball, etc. It took some time to find a doctor. In the meantime the poor guy was moaning in pain. The fellow's buddy, the one who brought him in, was getting increasingly agitated, especially since the medic on duty didn't seem to give a darn whether the man was suffering from pain or not. In fact I don't think he did give a darn. He was a good medic but had seen so much suffering and pain that he finally had become immune to it. Finally the buddy blurted out, "Can't you see he's in pain? Aren't you going to do something about it?" The medic's response was, "You know, I can't feel a thing, and, no, I am not going to do anything. He'll just have to wait until the doctor arrives." I thought the buddy was going to slug him. It seemed to me he could have at least given him some demoral to deaden the pain. But at the same time, demoral is a narcotic, and he might have gotten himself in trouble had he administered it without a doctor's permission. Poor guy, I felt so sorry for him. I am sure he was one G.I. who wished he never had talked himself into having the circumcision. Oh, yes, a doctor finally arrived. The patient was taken into surgery, the area to be sutured was deadened, and for the second time the sutures were put in place.

SPRING 1954

The signs of spring were now more evident. What few trees there were, were budding. The low places were showing some green, as were the hillsides. "Hon, you should see the rice paddies, they are stacked in a terrace-like arrangement. The arrangement is from the top of the hill or mountain to the bottom. Not an acre of land is left idle, what can be put to the plough is put to use. You may be wondering where the water comes from since I have previously mentioned that water in the mountains is very scarce. Well, that's a good question since I really don't know where the water comes from. Of course, there are the periodic heavy rains but as the rice matures the paddies have to be immersed in water. Somehow the farmers find a spring or small stream and directs its flow to the upper most paddy. Once that paddy is full, it flows to the next lower down and then to the next until all have been filled. Since no machinery is needed for the planting and harvesting of rice, the steep inclines present no problem. In mid summer the Korean country side is picturesque and beautiful."

The spring of 1954 was very reminiscent of the spring of 1953. There was constant alteration between warm days, some very warm, and cold days, some very cold. And the rains came and great was their coming. At times it would rain for up to two days without let up. Fortunately, at Clearing Company 2nd Medical Battalion, unlike the 120th Clearing Company of the 45th Division, mud was not a problem. What was a problem, however, was the incessant wind. There were few days when it didn't blow and blow hard. This was such a contrast to the Takkal-Li and Ko Ban Sang Ni areas that we occupied when I was with the 45th. In those mountain valleys, the wind seldom blew. In addition, the soil was much different. I would classify it as black loam. When it was wet we had endless seas of mud. The texture of the soil on the land occupied by the 2nd Division was mostly sand, and when the wind blew, the sand blew with it. It got into the tents, into one's clothing, hair, eyes, and mouth. As previously mentioned, the 2nd Division was located in the Ch'orwon Valley area. Some said this valley, weather wise, was rather freakish. However, its average temperature was the warmest in Korea. In spite of the sandy soil, the relatively warm weather and abundant rain was ideal for farming and raising crops. In a very real way it's the breadbasket of Korea.

From time to time I saw farmers and their families moving up past the Company area on their way to abandoned rice paddies. They were now allowed to move closer to the D.M.Z. (Demilitarized Zone). As they went by, it was apparent they had little in the way of material goods. Most all their worldly possessions were hauled in one cart pulled by the farmer himself. Many found their houses destroyed and, until they could rebuild, they were given used Army squad tents in which to live. The Koreans were undoubtedly the hardest working people with whom I ever came into contact. Without draft animals, all labor was done by hand. The people were engaged in an occupation that their ancestors most likely had pursued for centuries. They certainly knew what they were doing, for in a relatively short time the rice paddies added a touch of green to the otherwise drab countryside.

"Preparing the rice paddies for planting is a most interesting procedure to watch. First of all, by means of irrigation the acres of rice paddies are flooded. The farmers then go into the paddies bare footed, with trousers rolled up, and hoe the ground until it is loosened. Then they walk around the ponds and push their legs down into the mud as far as they can. It seems everyone works. Why not? Their very survival depends on harvesting a crop…Its raining and the one paddy I have been watching is almost over flowing with water. The rains have to come and flood the fields for the harvest to be successful. I even saw an old Papa Sahn in the paddy, dressed completely in white with his tall black hat, skin the color of bronze and wearing the long white beard that characterizes the old grand pappies...I saw one mother carrying a baby on her back swing it to the front of her body, scoop up a couple of hands full of that filthy water in the paddy and gave it to her baby to drink. Small wonder the doctors say 'They all have intestinal parasites.'"

Following the architectural design common to Korea, the engineers of each division were busy building entire villages for the Koreans. Before leaving the 45th Division, a very attractive village had been almost completed. The 2nd Division was also building a village. Because it was time to go to work in the rice fields, the farmers began to stream into the area from points further to the south. Since no houses had yet been built in the village for the people, the Army either lent or gave them squad tents that were about worn out. I don't know what the people streaming back into the countryside would have done without Army squad tents. Soon, within the confines of the village, tents could be seen everywhere. The standing joke among the men in the Company was that in the village there were 4000 prostitutes and 40 Mama Sahns in control of them. An exaggeration to be sure, but once again the hills were full of prostitutes. After all, it was spring.

Wherever a number of squad tents were thrown up, there was a village and each varied in size. A short distance from the compound was a tent village that had at least three to four hundred people living within its borders. A bit farther down the road was another village, a very small one holding about four or five families of 25 to 35 people. Although size varied, one constant was the filth. It seemed that every village I saw was filthy. I do not mean to be casting dispersions on the Korean villagers, but it seemed to me that with a little effort the living sites could have been cleaned up. Perhaps living in a tent provided no incentive to do so. Did the people live this way before the war when they lived in established villages of long standing? Or when they lived on individual farms, before they had to be squeezed into a tent village limited in space? It was clear to me how the conditions within the tent villages could easily breed communicable diseases.

March not only marked the arrival of spring, but the11th also marked the celebration of my first full year in Korea. It had been just a year since I had arrived at Inchon and made the amphibious landing, having no idea where the enemy was. I recalled the shore batteries pounding away and the constant flight of planes, diving and strafing. I recalled the cold train ride to Yo'ngdong P'o on the slow moving train believing the enemy was just over the hills. It wasn't until the following day I learned that the action over and around Inchon was an exercise. We were kept in the dark on purpose, of that I am sure. Particularly depressing was the number of men that boarded the landing crafts to return to the ship. These men had served their time in Korea and were rotating back to the States. Here I was just starting my tour of duty in Korea, and they had completed theirs. It did not make for feelings of elation. It was also 13 months to the day that Bonnie and I said our goodbyes in her apartment in Omaha where I boarded a train for the ride to Camp Stoneman. Now, most of my tour of duty in Korea was behind me. I would soon be boarding a landing craft for a ride out to a ship for the return trip to the States while the men getting off the ship would just be starting their tour of duty in Korea. That hardly seemed possible.

Easter Sunday came on March 18th in 1954, and though I wanted to go to Easter services, I had to work instead. It was a real disappointment. Just a year earlier I had taken in two services, one at the 120th Clearing company and the other at one of the tank units where the Division Chief of Chaplains delivered an Easter message. I must admit, that on March 18th it was hard to get into the Easter spirit. There was nothing to remind me of Easter except the day on the calendar, yet I tried to prepare myself spiritually. I can't recall why someone wouldn't fill in for me while I went to the service. Could be that a good number of men were in Seoul for the day. The Army considered itself very lenient about allowing men to attend religious services

"It is a lovely spring Sunday, so this morning I decided to take a hike around the outer perimeter of the company area. My destination was one of the fields that had been burned some weeks earlier. It looked like a typical battleground. There were empty shell casings, cartridges, unexploded hand grenades, barbed wire entanglements and wreckage all over the place. I hadn't noticed this when the field was covered with high brown grass. As I wandered farther from the company area, I climbed a rather high hill, lay back and just enjoyed the scenery. It was one of the few times I was able to get away by myself. I had purchased a pair of binoculars while on R.&.R. and had them with me. As I was glassing off into the distance, I saw a small group of Korean women looking for and digging out the roots of plants and gathering whatever else they could find to eat. Again, I am reminded just how traditional Korea is. Particularly regarding the sharp division between male and female roles. Of course both men and women plant rice. Whereas I saw only the men preparing the fields for planting, I saw only women engaged in gathering activities. Men, of course, do the heavy labor. They have a device called an A Frame, which they carry on their backs at an angle. It is called an A Frame because it is shaped like an A. There is a shelf like affair attached to the top and bottom, and on these they pile no end of wood, furniture, straw or whatever they need to haul. I have seen men carrying loads that were stacked twice as high as they were tall. I never did see a woman carry an A Frame."

I stayed on my perch as long as I could before returning to the Clearing Company area. I guess I was taking a chance, though I walked slowly and watched in front of me, because there were still unexploded land mines in the area. Nonetheless, it was darn good to get away from the Company area for a spell even though it was risky and brief."

One thing I noticed was the complete absence of songbirds in Korea. It seemed so unusual. Here it was spring, a time when the air should have been filled with the songs of birds. But there was nothing but silence. I had been watching for cuckoos, but I had not see a single one. They couldn't have all been killed during the war. Birds are migratory creatures and, even if many were killed, birds should have been migrating in. One morning I did hear a cuckoo singing its haunting melody. However, I was unable to locate it. The bird's song reminded me of that of the mourning dove. The bird was close but the song sounded as if it were coming from a distance.

"With the return of spring, it isn't only the prostitutes that have returned to the area but armed bandits as well. They hit our company last night. They looted the tents, taking billfolds, radios, cameras, anything they could get their hands on. They came when everyone was asleep and walked right into the tents and carried out their thievery without waking anyone. It gives me the creeps knowing they can come into a tent and loot it without waking anyone. As a consequence, we will be pulling guard all night in the tent. Each of us, and there are eight, will take a one hour shift. I wonder what the bandits will do if someone awakenes while they are looting the tent? In order to get to the tents, they have to work their way through barbed wire and past the guards. I don't like to say it but this kind of thievery is a problem with potentially serious consequences. Perhaps a couple of them need to be caught in the act of stealing and shot. That should give all of them pause to think about the risk they are taking"

We were seeing an increasing number of men with V.D., however, not all were getting it from the girls in the hills. "With the truck going to Seoul every Sunday, there are guys in the Company that make the trip weekly in order to have sex with the prostitutes in Seoul. You know what I've been thinking. Since the men are not going to be denied sex with the prostitutes, the escalating V.D. rate suggests that it might be wise for the Army to set up a place for prostitutes, clean them up and keep them clean. The guys are going to have sex regardless. There is no doubt this would cut down on the V.D. rate as well as on the number of AWOLs. (absent without leave.) Of course the men would have to be tested before having sex with the girls. I find it surprising that I am even thinking this way since it sounds like I am endorsing immorality and I guess I am. But the way it is now is not the answer either. Wouldn't this cause an uproar back home? Oh, yes, I must tell you this. This morning a fellow came on sick call and tested positive for gonorrhea. After I received the result of his lab test, I asked him, Did you get it from a girl in Seoul or up in the hills? He smiled and replied, 'You may not believe this, but I got it from a Red Cross girl.' For some reason I was not surprised. Some time after the cease-fire, Red Cross women started showing up, morale boosters they were supposed to be though I didn't find them that way. It didn't take long before they had a pretty negative reputation. And of course, not being in the Army, they could fraternize with the enlisted men as well as the officers. I guess in the final analysis I can only conclude that they, like the men, also have sexual needs desiring satisfaction. I didn't think to ask the fellow if he had to pay the woman."

Because of the high incidence of V.D., MASH conducted a V.D. study. A number of men testing positive for gonorrhea were going to the hospital daily for a smear and penicillin shot. By daily testing and penicillin shots, the men could be determined to be free of the bacterium gonococcus or not. Frankly, I believed it to be an exercise in futility. I did not expect to see a decrease in V.D. cases, ever. Even if all the infected prostitutes had been cleaned up, infected G.Is. would quickly reinfect them. And had the infected G.Is. all been cleaned up, they would have quickly been reinfected by the prostitutes. The Army may have been able to keep tabs on the G.Is., though that is doubtful, especially with frequent AWOLs. However, it had no idea how many prostitutes there were and where all of them were located since they were scattered throughout the hills. How many times did I say it? When there are males and females, there will be sex no matter what the men have to do to get it. The attraction between the sexes is just too great for it to be otherwise. How naive', how very naive' on the part of the Army to believe that this attraction could be eliminated. So it was another study. For what? At the same time, I guess it should be given credit for trying. Again I found myself wondering if the idea I shared with Bonnie might not have had an impact on the incidence of V.D. I didn't believe then and I don't believe now that anyone wants to contract V.D.. If the G.Is. had a place to go where they knew the girls were not infected, I was and am almost certain they would have preferred them to the girls in the hills who, almost assuredly, were infected by the gonorrhea gonoccous. In a recent issue of U.S. News and World Report, I read a news item that made me sit up and take notice; "Sex is a fact of life in the military so the Army has moved to make it safe. Soldiers have been receiving a brochure on condoms and directions on how to use them…" (1/14/2000, P. 6) I guess men in the Army need to be thankful for small changes. It appears it took at least 50 years for the Army to take this small step.

One morning, a Captain was brought to E.R. with a self-inflicted gunshot wound. This raised quite an uproar since officers just do not go around shooting themselves. The way I heard it, he was cleaning his 45 automatic pistol. After he had finished, he inserted a loaded clip, pulled back the slide, and let it slam forward in order to see that it was functioning properly. He must have forgotten that the clip he inserted was loaded, and thinking the chamber was empty, pulled the trigger. BANG! He shot a hole in his left hand. It may have been accidental, but at the same time, it was also an act of extreme carelessness. He should have known better than to point the pistol at his hand under any circumstances. As I stated earlier, it is doubtful that some of the officers who carried a pistol daily knew from which end of the weapon the bullet exited. It reminded me of Dr. Gaddis, who was with us for a short time at the 120th Clearing Company. Now Dr. Gaddis must have thought the Company area was the O.K. Corral. Wherever he went, his 45 automatic went with him. He didn't wear it on his webbed pistol belt like most officers but rather in a leather holster on a leather belt that hung a good ways down his right leg. I can see him even now, strutting across the compound, his dark sunglasses perched on his nose, his pistol strapped to his right leg, and his field cap worn at a cocky angle. I will say this, however: he did provide us with some much-needed humor. He was one of the few doctors who even carried a pistol.

ON THE HUNT FOR THE ELUSIVE HEMORRHAGIC FEVER CARRIERS

One of the signs of the nearness of spring was the appearance of G.Is. on sick call with hemorrhagic fever and malaria. Again, all troops started on a regimen of chloroquin for malaria but there was no known defense against H.F. One just hoped and prayed that whatever the mite was that carried the disease, and it was believed the carrier was a mite, would not bite. In addition to the non-availability of a defense for H.F., there was still no known treatment or cure for those coming down with the disease. Some men would get extremely ill, some would die.

The Army was concerned enough about H.F. that a special hospital was set up for the sole purpose of treating those contracting the disease. I don't recall reading about or hearing about any research being done to determine what might constitute successful treatment. Thus, I assumed what would be going on at the hospital would be experimental in nature. Since it was believed a mite transmitted the disease the war to rid the area of the mites was on. The first victims of the war were pet dogs. The Division Surgeon was so convinced that dogs were hosts for the mite that it was decided to rid the area of all dogs. Now we had two dogs in our tent. One was a mongrel, a most gentle and pleasant dog to have around, that we named Tiger. In addition, we had a cute pup that was mostly brown with white markings on her face. We named the pup Dink. Dink was sheer joy to have around, a typical pup. She would race all over the place and was, without a doubt, a real moral booster. Unfortunately, we didn't get to keep Dink very long. One evening when we returned to the tent, both Tiger and Dink were gone. Tiger was killed. However, we later discovered that

166

Dink was taken by an officer for his personal pet. How small, how very small. The enlisted men were not allowed to keep their dogs, however, this particular officer not only absconded with Dink but also kept her. On the positive side, at least Dink wasn't put to death.

There were a lot of pet dogs in the outfit and all would have to go. It is possible all of the dogs were destroyed. It is also possible they were given to the indigenous Korean personnel who worked in the compound and lived in a nearby camp. Koreans ate dog meat, so it is possible that many of those dogs ended up in a stew pot. For the short time we had Tiger and Dink, we always made sure they were in the tent for the night. The Koreans were not above skulking around the tents looking for dogs, and if they found any running loose, they would take them. Oh yes, out of the generosity of the big hearts of the powers that be, at the last minute it was decided that two dogs would be allowed to remain in the Company area. What happened at Clearing Company happened throughout the Division.

When the rate of H.F. cases continued unabated, it was decided that dogs were not host carriers of the mite. Little good that did for our dogs since all but two, and Dink, had been destroyed or given to the Koreans.

Next it was believed that rodents were the hosts to the mite. Since there were many rats in the area, they were the next targets. In an attempt to rid the area of rats, the grass around the Company area was set on fire, a fire that soon got completely out of control, racing many miles away from the area toward the mountains. In fact, the fire almost burned the surgical wing of the hospital. At night we could see it's glow in the distance way up on the top of a low mountain. The fire raged and smoked through the nearby mountains for several days before finally burning itself out. As the fire went racing along, we could hear many rounds of ammunition going off as well as a few hand grenades and land mines. Any moron could have told the officers that hatched up that idea, that with the wind blowing as it was, the fire was going to get out of hand.

There was in the Company, a Captain White, an inveterate souvenir hunter. The ashes had barely cooled when the Captain was out in the darkened fields looking for souvenirs. He looked for souvenirs such as shell casings, cartridges, and weapons of any kind. I don't believe many weapons were left lying around. As the Captain walked about, he kicked at every piece of metal he could see. He was just lucky that one of those pieces of metal was not the trigger to a landmine, for had it been, his souvenir hunting days would have ended abruptly.

Again, as it turned out, rats alone were not the hosts to the mites whose bite caused H.F. since we continued to see cases right up to the time I rotated home. And still there was no defense against it nor treatment when it was contracted.

After the attempt to rid the Company area of possible mite carrying critters, Dr. Spicer gave a class on the three worst diseases one could catch in Korea. The first was hemorrhagic fever, and he reiterated in no uncertain terms that the medical profession didn't really know what caused it. Although they believed it was due to the bite of a certain mite, at the time doctors had not the slightest inkling how to cure it. Second was intestinal parasites, which are ingested from drinking water from streams and pools and from eating food that has been contaminated by unclean hands. Because of the use of human feces as fertilizer, any water draining into streams was contaminated. Since Koreans neither liked to bathe nor wash their hands, any food handled by them was likely to be contaminated by spores of the parasites. In fact, it was believed by the doctors that almost all Koreans had intestinal parasites. The intestinal parasites the Koreans had most often were 1) hookworms, 2) ascoriasis and 3) amebiasis.

I couldn't help recall a G.I. who had been up high in the mountains and came upon a stream gushing out of the ground. The water was cold and crystal clear. Feeling certain there was no way it could be contaminated, he took a long drink from the spring and within a few hours was suffering from stomach cramps and diarrhea. One could not be too careful around Korean food and surface as well as underground water.

The third disease Dr. Spicer covered was malaria. The worst in Korea being plasmodium vivax. At the same time, it was rarely fatal. With extreme caution, the intestinal parasites could be avoided, but there was no way to guard against H.F. and malaria. Not a very encouraging talk to hear with only two and one-half months left in Korea.

Although Dr. Spicer didn't mention it, rather alarming was the number of G.Is. being evacuated with tuberculosis. For a long time, the only victims of T.B. were Orientals. That was changing. Since Koreans and Americans lived in the same squad tents, it was almost impossible not to come into contact with someone who had active T.B. Working in the hospital and frequently being around T.B. patients caused me growing concern. I decided that before leaving for home, I would go over to the MASH for a chest X-Ray. I had that X-Ray and it proved to be negative for T.B. I was most thankful for that.

Another cause of death, not as frequent as H.F., but frequent enough, was the Korean liquor that was available outside the Company area. In fact, outside the entrance gate to the area was a sign that gave the number of G.Is. from the Division who had died from drinking Korean liquor.

The Koreans, always clever people, would hi-jack a truck carrying American liquor, drill a very small hole in the bottom of the bottles, drain out the good booze, and then refill the bottle with the concoction they made. Then they would seal the hole with some kind of wax. Lord only knows what was in their liquor. The entire Company was given a demonstration of how the Koreans accomplished this task. In addition, a number of bottles of confiscated Korean liquor were lined up on a table, and it was pointed out that if one looked carefully, he could see that no two bottles were filled to exactly the same level, as was the case with American or Canadian liquor. So, many unsuspecting G.Is. bought from the Koreans what they believed to be good American or Canadian whiskey or scotch. Later, much to their dismay and often agony, they discovered that what they had purchased was poison. The message seemed clear: woe unto he who had any vices for if he wasn't extremely careful, they were going to get him.

A Short Timer

It was now May, and I was what was called a "short timer." That meant that it would be a short time before I rotated home. Maybe that is what I was classified as, but for some reason, I didn't feel like a short timer. Most of my time had been served in Korea, yet I felt that the time remaining was interminably long. So far, the time of my departure had not changed. I checked on this frequently and was always assured that the dates were set, either May 21st or 27th. I was hoping it would be the former rather than the latter. Unfortunately, it didn't turn out that way. For the life of me, I am still unable to figure out why my friends at 2nd Division Clearing Company, were leaving before me. These were friends who were drafted the same time as I, started basic training at the same time, came over on the same ship, arrived on Korean soil the same day and yet were leaving for home anywhere from two to three weeks in advance of me. There had to be a reason. The last word was I had three or four weeks to go before I would rotate. My rotation date had been pushed back so often, and my hopes had been dashed so many times that perhaps this was why I did not feel like a short timer. The projected date of my departure could be changed again. And, it was. In a short time, I was notified that at best it would not be before the first week in June, most likely the 10th.

I drove down to the Personnel Section at Division Rear and raised hell. I told anyone who would listen that based on earlier assurances Bonnie and I had set our wedding date for the 27th of June. If I started processing for rotation on the 10th of June, I would never make it home in time for my own wedding. I also told them that if they held me until the 10th of June, I might not get home in time to be accepted for the fall semester at the University of South Dakota, where I had decided to pursue my education. It was all to no avail. I was told that a recent 8th Army order stated that no men who were on the point system would rotate prior to 102 days before their discharge. I had 118 days left on the 21st of May and 108 days left on the 31st of May. Because of a mere six days, my stay in Korea had again been extended. But what about my friends who either had left for home or who were leaving for home shortly? I was told that my case had no bearing on them. Damn Army.

The one bright part of the ever-changing dates was that when I got back to the States, instead of being reassigned for two months of stateside duty, I would be discharged. At the time this seemed small compensation. What loomed large was getting caught in what seemed like never ending changes.

Now that my letters were filled with the anticipation of home coming, agreeing to the finalization of wedding plans Bonnie had made, the excitement over the return of spring, etc., she wanted to know what Army life in Korea was like. In one of her letters she suggested it would be better if I told her while I was still in Korea, still living the life. It was a question to which no quick answers came. I had to give it some thought. I wrote her that letter and 45 years later, as I read and re-read my responses to her question, and now looking back after almost 50 years, I don't think there would be much that I would change.

"My home here in the Army consists of a space 7 X 4 feet in size, containg my cot, a foot locker, a shelf and space under the cot. There is absolutely no privacy; I am almost never alone. The only privacy I have is my thoughts and feelings. I sleep, eat, work, play and exist with the other men in the Company. Eight or nine of us live in the squad tent, which is 16 feet wide and 32 feet long. We all share the same washstand, two washbasins, and one table on which we either write letters or play cards. We each have about 120 pounds of clothing hung or stored in our little 7 X 4 floor space. Three-hundred and fifty of us share the same shower and the same mess hall. There are many different personalities in a tent of seven other fellows, and I have to adjust to all seven in such a way that our relationships are harmonious. Frequently squabbles do arise over things that others might consider unimportant but often become explosive because of the tension created by the many months of continuous confinement and the idiocy of the Army. Three or four of the fellows come in drunk and noisy. Well, what can I say; this tent is as much their home as mine.

All 350 of us fall out for formation. We aren't Cabral, Withrow, Garzon or Waltner. No, we are numbers 15, 16, 17 and 18 respectively. It is only that deeply entrenched self image that reminds each and every one of us that we are individuals. Over time, some fellows lose even that and their self then becomes one with the Army. We live under the constant strictures of authority, and punishment for infractions is often severe. Since we live in a world of propaganda, there really is no peace of mind. Our newspaper, The Stars and Stripes, Far East Edition, is full of propaganda as are all radio stations. We are kept tense, nervous and a bit frightened. Frightened? Yes, frightened. The latest rumor is that with the conflict at Dien Bien Phu, French Indo China, all enlistments will be frozen and rotation to the States will be curtailed. The American Army in Korea will board ships and travel south to become embroiled in that conflict. Since there is no denial of these rumors, I would imagine the Army is really not interested in debunking them."

We didn't go from Korea to Dien Bien Phu to French Indo China, as it was called then. However, about one decade later the United States began to involve itself in that part of the world militarily, and eventually that involvement led to the Vietnam War.

"We do have freedom of thought, thank God, though I dare say that if the Army could take that from us, it would. There is strict limitation of expression and movement and immediately a conflict arises between mind and body. Every phase of military life requires a different type of adjustment. The majority of fellows make a survivable adjustment even if it is buying into the Army, hook, line and sinker. Those who can't make the adjustment often end up in the N.P. (neuropsychiatric) ward for a spell.

Let me say this, the Army is the most dictatorial, totalitarian institution I have ever encountered and ever hope to encounter. And it seems such a contradiction since we are over here to prevent South Korea from falling into the hands of a dictatorial and totalitarian regime.

Well, Sweetheart, so much for an insight into what Army life is like. At least this is my perception and, for sure, everyone does not share it. I have seen much and learned much. And hopefully, in the years ahead as I reflect on all this, I will acquire even more understanding. However, now the important thing is that I get home to you just as quickly as I can."

The Army always operates by the rules. It doesn't make any difference if those rules make sense at the time or not. On May 11, because that was the set date, we turned in all of our winter gear including our winter sleeping bags. It made no difference that we had some very chilly, cold days ahead of us. It made no difference that sleeping, in particular, would be very difficult if not impossible on some nights. Winter clothing and sleeping bags would be turned in on the 11th. Already our stoves had been taken out so when it did turn cold, there was no way of heating the tent. Days weren't so bad; it was the nights that were so uncomfortable. Now, a summer weight sleeping bag is a bag made out of the equivalent of a G.I. blanket and nothing more. There were nights when I got very little sleep because of the cold. But rules were rules and, once made they were set in stone.

On May 18th, an exercise named "Operation George" was held. Jets and conventional planes buzzed around, artillery pounded, and helicopters fllew overhead, causing me concern that the shooting on the M.L.R. had once again started up. I was getting so close to rotation that I had a dread of that happening. I knew that if it did, rotation home would come to an end. As it turned out, it was a practice alert and carried out to impress Secretary of Defense Charles (Choo Choo) Wilson, who was reviewing the military strength of the 8th Army on line and in reserve. It is to be remembered that the 2nd Division was still on line. So Operation

George was a reaction to a mock enemy attack. The alert started at 9:00 a.m. and continued until 2:00 p.m.

One morning a couple of men from the Battalion brought in a little Korean girl who had been hit in the head by a flying tin can. Just outside our barbed wire enclosure was a trash dump. These men were over by the dump unloading some trash. The dump was right next to the small Korean village mentioned earlier. All of the little tykes from the village came running when they saw the truck pull up. In the process of unloading the truck, the little girl was hit by a flying tin can. She had quite a nasty cut on top of her head. We cleaned it up, shaved around it, and then took her into surgery where Jim and I put in a few sutures. What a cute and brave little girl. She was crying a little when she first came into the E.R., perhaps more from fright than pain. However, she didn't so much as whimper when we deadened the area around the wound. After we finished suturing the wound, I washed her face and hands, which were so very, very dirty. She left Clearing Company with a box filled with candles, candy bars, gum, etc. I said it many times. The American G.I. has to be the most generous person. All of us kind of fell for the little tyke. She was such a cute little girl. I figured her to be eight or nine years old. I was wrong, she told our interpreter she was 13. I found that hard to believe but, as previously mentioned, it was very difficult to accurately guess the age of Koreans, even the little ones.

Jim and I were friends, a friendship that extended back to the beginning of basic training. Sometime after Ken and I were transferred to the 2nd Division, Jim was also transferred to the 2nd. Back during basic, Jim was in love, head over heels in love. He and his fiancé were married during the brief furlough from Camp Pickett to Camp Stoneman. When we got to Korea, both of us, along with Ken, were assigned to the 45th Division. Initially, Jim's wife wrote him twice a day. The outside of the envelopes were plastered with stick-on hearts, rabbits, and other reminders of her love for Jim.

Now Jim was a frugal man, keeping only a few dollars from his monthly income and sending the rest home to his wife. Often I would loan him a few dollars until payday. Within a couple of months, the two letters per day became one letter. A couple of months later, they came at the rate of about three a week. Later they arrived unpredictably. Jim would often talk to me about what was happening to his wife. He suspected that another man had come into her life; in fact, she intimated as much in one of her, by this time, infrequent letters. Such a letter came to be referred to as a "Dear John Letter." In fact, they came so frequently to Korea, that Homer and Jethro put together a song entitled, "Dear John." One line I remember because I thought it funny was "Please send me my auto-graphed picture of Roy Acuff cause my husband wants it now." The song may have been a spoof, but there was nothing funny about Dear John letters. This upset Jim to no end but, although he tried to get an emergency leave in order to go home in an effort to put his faltering marriage back together, the request for a leave was denied.

One quiet evening in E.R., Jim started crying the blues. He had been so faithful sending his money to his wife. When he returned home, they would have a nice little nest egg on which to begin their lives together. Jim was also a sergeant, and way back then a sergeant made a whopping $160.00 per month. Instead of saving the money, his wife was spending it all. He showed me a letter he had received in which she informed him that she had just spent $400.00 on a TV set, $200.00 on a wrist watch and hundreds more on other items; including an exorbitant amount on an Indian throw rug. She had mentioned in a previous letter that she wanted a watch. Jim wrote her to hold off a bit before buying one since he could get her a very good Gruen or Bulova in the P.X. for around $40.00. She couldn't wait; she had to have it now.

During our conversation, Jim said to me, "Dick, I think I am going to re-enlist and extend my tour of duty in Korea. I really no longer have any-thing to go home to. My wife has spent about everything I sent home, and she has let on that she is seeing another man." Now Jim didn't care for the

Army and I was surprised to hear him talking about re-enlisting. I encouraged him to give it much thought before he took that step. Poor Jim. Just a few months earlier, he had been head over heels in love with his wife and she, at least it appeared, was in love with him.

Jim, however, was legion. I knew several men whose marriages ended while they were in Korea. Men who like Jim were married during their brief furlough between Camp Pickett and wherever it was they shipped out for Korea. At most this would give the couples three or four days together, and this was after 16 weeks of separation during basic training. For a time I shared a squad tent with one of these men back at the 120th Clearing Company. He was about to go on R.&.R. and confided in me that he was going to "shack up with a Japanese prostitute." I was surprised and said something to the effect, "But how can you do that, you just got married a few months ago?" "Hell," he replied, "she's stepping out on me." Absence makes the heart grow fonder? Sorry, in so many cases, it just wasn't so. The "Dear John" letter was no myth.

On the morning of May 23rd, Ken Worthington left for Division Rear, then to Pusan and from there home, which was Oregon City, Oregon. He was scheduled to ship out on either the 28th or 29th. Then Jim received his rotation orders for the 2nd of June. Though I was happy for them, I was sorry to see both of these men leave. Almost two years earlier, the three of us began basic training at Camp Pickett, Virginia. Other than the short time when Jim was absent from Clearing Company, 2nd Division, we had been together. When Jim left, I was the only one of the original "old timers" left in the Company. At this point I can only say that I was even more bitter at the Army. Why I was still in Korea I didn't know and I never found out. Ken, Jim and I had exactly the same number of rotation points, yet they would be gone and I would still be at the Clearing Company. Jim had decided to wait until he had a chance to talk to his wife before making a decision on re-enlisting. I often wondered how that turned out.

My "window of opportunity" to rotate was between June 1st and June 10th. Assuming I would not be extended again, that meant in just 8 days I would enter my rotation period. I was both anxious and cautious.

"Dr Lee examined a Korean baby, suspicious that the infant had hydrocephalus. However, after he reviewed the case, he changed his diagnosis. Now he believes the baby definitely has rickets and not hydrocephalus. Such a cute baby and so small. I couldn't believe it when the mother said the child was three years old. That is a bit misleading, for in the Orient an individual is one year old at the time of birth, which means that by the way we measure age in the West the child was only two years old. The child was three years old, and here I thought she was a baby, at most six or seven months old. Dr. Lee has put the baby on hexavitamins, with instructions for the mother to return with the baby. However, that will not happen. This afternoon an order came down from Division Headquarters that the medical facilities were not to see nor treat any more Korean personnel. I don't know if it has anything to do with it, but General Seitz doesn't like Clearing Company."

The mother returned the next day with her baby but had to be turned away. She was completely perplexed. Not being able to speak nor understand English, she was unable to understand why she would not be admitted to the compound, especially when the doctor told her to return. Dr. Lee threw up his hands in total exasperation since he was sure he could have helped the baby if just given the chance. The child did not get the treatment it so badly needed, but obviously the Army didn't care. Nothing unusual, just another example of ugly Americans.

We had a big Company formation the morning of May 29th. And, of course, we heard the same old crap from Sergeant Dunn. He got up on his stool and yelled; "You guys are men, you're soldiers and you are supposed to act like soldiers." I can't remember what was bugging him. Who was he trying to kid? Real men wouldn't take that crap, they would rebel. Many are broken down and defeated. How is one supposed to act like a man when treated like men in skirts? Further, I felt the men had been conducting themselves remarkably well, given the routine and monotony of life in Korea, especially life in a forward division. One thing is sure. It took a certain kind of personality to make a career out of the military and most men didn't have that kind of personality.

Bob Withrow and I had become good friends. Bob had been with the 2nd Clearing Company since his arrival in Korea. We had a lot in common and spent many hours discussing issues of concern to both of us. Bob was married and I am sure he missed his wife Shirley as much, if not more, as I missed Bonnie. He was scheduled to rotate home on the 29th of May, nine days before I would leave the Company. As with Ken and Jim, Bob had been drafted and he had begun basic the same time I did, however, he would be leaving and I would remain for a bit longer. On the morning of the29th, we said our good byes with my promise that Bonnie and I would find our way out to San Jose before too many years went by. And we did. In August of 1956 we spent a delightful week with Bob and Shirley.

"June 1, and the first day of my rotation period. I have just 10 days in which to be informed that I have been placed on orders to rotate. It seems I am more nervous than ever, Hon. Although I am generally a stranger to depression, I feel somewhat depressed when actually I should be elated. I'm concerned that the powers that be may louse things up or that I will be extended again. It has happened so often that I don't think I am being unrealistic. And, after all, points or no points, my two years won't be up until September 17th. I suppose the Army could keep me in Korea until shortly before my discharge date. It is also an uncomfortably cool day with rain threatening. It is getting to be that time of spring when the heavy rains fall. Although the ground around here is sandy and we don't have the mud we had at Tokkal-Li and Ko Ban Sang Ne, no matter how one looks at it, mud is mud."

It seemed as if the Clearing Company was plagued with inspections. Inspections for this and inspections for that. Most of them were nonsense and little more than harassment. How many inspections were necessary to prove that a unit was battle ready and worthy? On June 3rd we had another impromptu inspection, this time by General Robinson, 8th Army Surgeon General. The inspection went off without a hitch. The Army just wouldn't be the Army without endless inspections. Major White, Battalion Commander, was the biggest chicken I had come across, especially when it came to Commanding General Seitz. The man was scared to death of Seitz. He began almost every sentence with, "The General said this, and the General said that." In fact, his nickname was "The General Said." In a way it was both amusing and disgusting. I guess he just didn't have much backbone. And it didn't help matters much for the Major that the General did not like the medics. I am sure he was much more concerned about inspections than were the enlisted men. Well, I had to admit that all that boot licking paid off for within a few days MajorWhite was promoted to Lieutenant Colonel.

"Here it is June 4th, with only six days left in my rotation period, and I am beginning to get more than a bit nervous. If those orders aren't received by the 10th, I have decided to see the Inspector General. It may not help but at least he can find out what is causing the delay. This is a lovely, melancholy day that makes me exceptionally lonely for you."

I was supposed to be rotating in a few days and still I was assigned as Sergeant of the Guard. It was a rainy night but not bad for me since I was inside most of the time. When I did check on my guards, I wore my raincoat. However, I could imagine how uncomfortable it was for the guards putting in a three-hour shift in the rain. Even though they also wore raincoats, their feet got wet. The three-hour shift was something new. The men had a choice of two two hour shifts or one three hour shift. Most chose the one three hour shift because when it was over they were through for the night. In addition, the number of guards posted had been reduced so fewer men were on guard. The period during which the area had to be guarded had also been shortened. It ran from 7:30 p.m. until 4:30 a.m. Clearly, the perception of a renewed outbreak of hostilities along the M.L.R. was diminishing.

June 7, 1954. "Three cheers, Hon, I finally made it. I'm so darn excited I can hardly write. The phone call just came in from Division Rear, and Spaulding rushed right over to tell me. There are five of us who will be leaving from the Battalion. Soon we will be together Darling and then our future together will begin. Right now I have to be the happiest guy in the world. I will leave Battalion on the morning of June 9th and will leave Division Rear on the morning of the 10th. Where I will board ship I do not know. Tomorrow I am just going to take it easy and pack up. Wednesday morning I will be leaving. The day we have been waiting for such a long time has finally arrived. Hon, I just can't hold my pen so guess I'd better quit for tonight. In 20 days, my Darling, we will be in each other's arms. Good night, Sweetheart, I love you so very much."

A Day in Seoul

Before leaving for home, I wanted to make one trip to Seoul. Clearing Company, 2nd Medical Battalion, started sending a two and one half ton open truck to Seoul every Sunday, commencing, I believe, in May. It was still cool and the ride in the back of the truck would be a dirty and dusty one. If I wanted to get to Seoul, I had no choice but to put up with the cold and the dirt. On Sunday, May 16, Bob Withrow and I hopped aboard the open truck and made the trip to Seoul.

The ride, as anticipated, was dusty and cold. We left in clean uniforms, looking real sharp. We looked like ghosts by the time we arrived in Seoul. Although we left the Company area at 8:30, it was 11:30 before we pulled into Seoul. Since the truck left for the Company area at 3:30, this would give us only four hours to see Seoul. Of course, once we stepped off the back of the truck, we were on foot.

One of the first things we found was a beautiful park with several pagoda like buildings. The grounds were well groomed and many Koreans were visiting the park. Most likely it was some kind of Buddhist shrine since it appeared obvious the North Koreans made no attempt to destroy it. As I looked at the many Koreans walking about the park, it became obvious to me that in spite of the recent war, there were still some wealthy Koreans. Some of the couples were very attractively dressed, and I also learned a good lesson. Earlier I commented that the Korean women I had seen were very plain looking and unattractive. However, as pointed out, they were farmwomen. In the park I saw many attractive and well dressed Korean women. I realized that all it took was a hairstyle other than being pulled back and knotted, a bit of make-up, and nice clothing to make some of the women most attractive. Also these were not farm women subject to the hard work and to the aging effects of the sun in which they seemed to be constantly working. Already back in 1954, the men were dressed in Western style business suits while the women were dressed in more traditional attire.

Downtown Seoul 1953

From the park, Bob and I walked a few side streets. It was on one of these side streets that we came upon the fruit vendor with the most delicious looking apples. It was after noon and many hours since we had eaten. Though the apples looked tempting, the fear of getting intestinal parasites at this late date was enough to cause us to keep walking, leaving the apples on the table.

One of the side streets took us close to the capital building. It was as I had seen it in March of 1953. No repairs whatsoever had been made. What caught my attention was a large and long banner hanging from the front of the capital building with the words, "Welcome Secretary of Defense Wilson." If my memory serves me correctly, Charles Wilson was President Eisenhower's Secretary of Defense. Apparently he was either in

Korea or about to pay Korea a visit. I often wondered if that building was ever restored or if a new site was chosen for the capital.

On another side street we came upon a scene that made a deep impression on me. My later training as a sociologist lent a much deeper meaning to what I saw. We encountered a group of young people who appeared to be horsing around and nothing more. Down the sidewalk apiece, we noticed a very old Papa Sahn dressed completely in white with white jacket and bloomer like trousers, save for his very tall black stovepipe hat. As he neared, we could see that he was walking as erect as a reed. When he was almost even with the young people, they stepped off the sidewalk into the gutter. As he passed, they bowed very low which I interpreted to be a gesture of respect. I thought to myself, how wonderful that, in Korea at least, having reached an advanced age was a badge of honor to be respected. This was just another example of how the traditional society was structured. Since few lived to an advanced age an elder was respected for having beat the odds that he wouldn't make it. What a contrast to the attitude towards age in the U.S., where the elderly are in the way and of little use. I can't imagine back in 1954 an elderly Korean being placed in an equivalent to an old people's home or nursing home. In American society today, it is becoming increasingly popular to warehouse the elderly and infirm. They are placed in old people's homes, nursing homes, minimum care facilities, maximum care facilities, etc. Whatever they are called, it is obvious that reaching old age is nothing to look forward to nor is it recognized as a badge of accomplishment. Can the reader see young people in America stepping off the street and bowing to an elderly person as he or she passes by? To be sure, that would be the day.

Bob and I also walked through what had been the main business district of Seoul. I guess it still would have been called the main business district. There were few shops. We did pass a couple that were selling garments made from G.I. clothing, sleeping bags, blankets, etc. Most likely the items were highjacked or purchased on the black market. It seemed that everyone on the street wore something O.D.(olive drab) in color. The Koreans would take the G.I. clothing apart, rip open the sleeping bag covers and make completely new outfits from them. In fact, I bought a waist length jacket made from some lightweight olive drab material. Even though it may very well have been made from stolen goods, when I wore it around the Clearing Company in the evenings, not a word was said.

This was May 1954, 14 months since my arrival in Korea. Seoul was dirty and over crowded, however, the people appeared content unlike in March of 1953 when I saw so much hunger. Although Bob and I encountered some begging, most of the people we saw looked quite well fed.

The four hours passed much too quickly, and at 3:30 we again boarded the truck for the long, cold ride back to Clearing Co. How could it take three and one half to four hours to drive 55 miles? The roads, the roads. In places, we just crawled along.

Even though it was cold and dirty, the ride back was interesting. We were now in the Ch'orwon Valley, a flat area, and there were rice paddies everywhere. The countryside was beginning to green up, and with a clear sky over head it was a lovely sight. I also discovered that rice wasn't the only crop raised by the Korean farmers. There were fields of oats and wheat. It seemed everyone was busy in the fields.

We drove through a couple of towns, P'och'on and Uijongbu. Uijongbu had been the scene of heavy fighting as the North Korean army swept south. In fact, all that was left of it was a sign indicating where the village had been. I had been told it was at Uijongbu that an Army or Marine unit heard voices but couldn't locate them. Since the voices continued, they kept looking and finally found the mouth of a cave that had been sealed by the North Koreans troops. They dug out the opening and inside the cave were several hundred people, almost the entire population of Uijongbu. They had been sealed in the cave and left to starve to death. They were in pretty tough shape but I believe most survived.

What wasn't so lovely was the constant odor of human feces. That is something I did not get used to. We got back to Clearing Co., tired and cold, but I was glad I made the trip since it was my only chance to see Seoul unimpeded by constant military supervision and surveillance. Oh yes, in spite of hearing so much about Seoul and it's prostitutes, we were not approached by any women wanting to sell us sex.

GOODBYE KOREA

I got up early on the morning of June 8th. Most of my clothing and equipment was packed. I had a small gym bag that I purchased in Japan for my personal effects. In fact, the bag held all of my personal effects, other items had already been sent home. It was amazing how easy it was to accumulate things; it didn't seem to matter where one was or what the circumstances were. I had purchased a Hallicrafters short wave radio from a friend who had rotated home earlier. Ordinarily I would have sold it, but radios of all description were now available at the P.X. and no one I knew was interested in a used Hallicrafters. It was a big machine, big because it took a big battery to run it. This was before transistors and small radios that ran on double A, triple A and 9-volt batteries. The battery compartment comprised most of the radio. I never was able to understand how such a big battery would last only two or three hours at most. I still have that radio and every once in a while I plug it in and let it play. Since it's a tube radio, it gets pretty noisy picking up all the static. Even with most of my personal possessions on the way home, my gym bag was still full. I would regret that when I got to Inchon.

The truck from Battalion Headquarters was to pick me up at 8:00 a.m, which meant I had to say my good byes early. As elated as I was, it was hard saying goodbye to my fellow sergeants with whom I shared the squad tent. Some pretty deep friendships can be formed in three months time. They were all glad for me. This time it was I saying goodbye and my friends were staying behind. They went to work and I sat alone on my duffel bag, by the side of the road, waiting for the truck to arrive. That's the way it was. Friendships were made and nurtured. When it came time

186

to say goodbye, there were hand shakes and well wishes and then everyone went about their business and we were never to see each other again.

The truck took me to Battalion without delay. I was taken directly to Division Rear, which was only a 10 minute ride. The first thing on the agenda was to turn in my field equipment. If anything was missing, I would be charged for it. Fortunately, nothing was. It was a good feeling to unload my field pack, shelter half, entrenching tool, etc. At that, it took most of the morning to get the gear turned in. The Army was most meticulous in checking each piece of equipment. During combat, that was not the way it was. It was easy to write off items as combat losses. As the 45th was being broken up, a fellow I knew walked into the tent and tried to sell me a new 45 automatic. He started at $10.00 and then dropped down to $5.00. Perhaps I could have packaged it up and sent it home and it would have made it without a hitch. However, to be caught doing such a thing was a court marshal offense and I wasn't about to run that risk. That 45 automatic, most likely, had been written off as a battle loss and no one was looking for it. He ended up walking a short distance up the side of the mountain behind the tent and throwing it into the bushes. He wasn't about to take a chance either. I really didn't care how long it took to turn in equipment. The Army set the schedule and the Army would have to meet it. My feeling was one of elation, like a ton had been taken off my shoulders. No more reveille, no more retreat, no more pesky impromptu inspections and soon, no more Army.

That evening I was given my shipping orders. I would be leaving from Inchon, and when I stepped on the ship, I would have come full circle. I would make the trip to Inchon from Division Rear, complete my processing and then board ship in a day or two. The Army seemed in a hurry to get the men processed and for a time I thought I just might get home a few days earlier than anticipated. Of course, it didn't turn out that way. There was no way I was going to get home a single day earlier than that date set by the Army

Early the morning of the 9th, 350 men from the 2nd Division jumped into trucks for a two-hour ride to a train depot where we would take yet another slow train ride for the last leg of the trip to Inchon. Everyone was in a good mood and why not? I wasn't the only one with 14 or 15 months served in Korea. Once again I found myself in "casual status," standing in long lines, making formations, etc. However, for once, I didn't mind it one bit.

On June 11th, after having written daily for 15 months, I wrote my last letter to Bonnie from Korea. "My Darling: Here I am at the Inchon Rotation Depot and the last 24 hours have been hours of rushing here and there. At 6:00 a.m. I took a truck to a nearby railhead where I boarded a train. Along the way to Inchon, we picked up troops from the 3rd and 7th Divisions. We really had a train full, about 900 men and all rotatees. The ride down here was quite pleasant. Hon, you just wouldn't believe how very much this country has changed in the past 15 months. It really is amazing. Fifteen months ago there were very few villages and the country-side was bare; there was no farming at all. Now the entire countryside is under cultivation and what an improvement that has made; it is even quite attractive. And with all the little villages springing up, it is really something to see.

I arrived here at the Depot at 12:00 noon, just in time for chow. After chow, the processing began. The first thing I did was to strip down to my boots and turn in all of my issued clothing. And what a rush that was. I was given a big box and into that I poured all of my stuff and Hon, in spite of all that I packed and sent home; I'm still traveling way to heavy. I never realized I had so darn much stuff. I had a heck of a time keeping my eyes on it at all times.

After I turned in my issued clothing, I then had my personal items checked. Next came a hot shower and after that I went down the line again. I was issued three pairs of shorts, two T-shirts, one raincoat, three pairs of socks, two fatigue uniforms and two dress khaki uniforms. In addition, I was issued a new duffel bag. Parting with the old one was like giving up a good friend. By the time I got through with all of this, I was about done in.

It was time for supper so I ate. Then it was time to have my Army records checked. That took awhile but everything was in order. After we finished with the records, we were billeted for the night. And what a short night it was. I was up bright and early the next morning and at it again. First thing on the morning agenda was an orientation about our voyage home, and Darling, this is the way it is to be. I will leave here tomorrow morning for Inchon Port and will immediately board ship. I suppose it will take a few hours to load all the troops. We are scheduled to set sail tomorrow. It will take approximately 14 days to cross the ocean. That is longer than I expected. The ship will dock at Fort Lewis, near Seattle, Washington. Hon, it is a good thing we didn't plan to meet on the coast because there will be no opportunity to see loved ones or friends. We will be rushed right on through at Fort Lewis.

Now Darling, I don't know if I am going to be able to get to a phone at Fort Lewis, but I will try my level best to phone you. If I can't, I will try to send you a telegram. I will do all that is in my power to contact you just as soon after landing as I can. I will be discharged from Camp Carson, Colorado. After debarking near Fort Lewis, I should be on my way to Carson in a matter of hours.

We were also informed that we would be discharged just as rapidly as possible. So Darling, perhaps by the time you get to Camp Carson, I should just about be out of the Army. I simply can't wait. I will be so happy when I can take you into my arms. Once I do I will never let you out of them. We can drive home together, and the time we spend on the road will be just great. No more goodbyes.

Well, Hon, I guess this will be my last letter from Korea, since I will board ship tomorrow. That day we have long been waiting for is finally just about here. I am eager and excited. I love you with all my heart. I will call you just as soon as it is humanly possible. It will be so wonderful to hear your voice. It won't be long now; it won't be long at all. I love you sweetheart. Soon we will be together and no more goodbyes. All my love."

The Army did a lousy job of outfitting me for the journey home. The under clothing and the fatigues were okay but the raincoat was about three sizes too large. But worst of all were the Khaki uniforms I would wear upon reaching Seattle. Neither uniform fit and, complain as I may, no changes would be made. One of the uniforms had been pressed on a piece of newspaper; the entire side of one of the pair of trousers was covered with newsprint that could not be removed. Fortunately, one of the fellows at Inchon Rotation Depot told me where I could find a good tailor. The moment I had a chance, I looked him up. Both pairs of trousers and both shirts had to be taken in. He assured me he would have them ready in a couple of hours and true to his word, they were ready. Better yet, he did an excellent job of alteration and they fit well. I didn't have to go home looking like Ichabod Crane. It seemed to me that the least the Army could have done is issue me presentable clothing. But why should I have expected that? I was the one who was at fault for thinking the Army would care how the troops looked once they stepped off the ship. Oh yes, I never did wear the trousers with the newsprint on the leg.

HOME AT LAST

On the morning of June 13, approximately 2,500 men boarded the Marine Serpent. No time was wasted. It took several hours to transport that many troops from shore to ship with landing crafts. However, as soon as all were aboard, the steel platform onto which we stepped to board the ship was taken up and the ship moved out of the bay.

As I watched Korea fade into the distance, I did so with feelings of mixed emotions. After all, it had been my home for 15 months and, though I detested the Army, I had come to appreciate Korea, perhaps to even love it a bit. I have seen many moonlit nights but none compared with those I saw in Korea. I can still see that purple haze, bright enough to illuminate the surrounding valleys, hillsides and mountains. I could not help but like the people, so patient and long suffering. They weren't all good people; to be sure, there were thieves and potential murderers that were encountered. It would only be later that I would fully appreciate what it meant to live among those people and to observe a traditional society. I fear it is traditional no longer. Of course, there would be pockets of traditionalism in the backcountry; however, today Korea is a thoroughly modern society. For years I had wanted to return for a visit, however, in recent conversation with a Korean engineer, who has been In the U.S. a few years, I was told that the Korea I remember no longer exists. For example, he told me that Ch'unch'on, which was not much more than a cardboard village in 1953/54, was now a thriving modern city linked to Seoul by a four-lane highway. He told me of many other changes, enough that I changed my mind about returning. From what he said, there would be nothing I would recognize.

I have but one regret. There were many orphans and I wanted to adopt a little girl. Initially Bonnie wasn't very enthused about the idea. Though I brought it up repeatedly for several years, she never warmed to the idea. Had she been more willing and had we adopted a little girl, I would have had my daughter.

From Korea, the Marine Serpent sailed to Yokohama, where it picked up additional troops rotating home from Japan. As soon as they were aboard, we again set sail. Docking in the harbor was an interesting experience for me. A tug came out, hooked onto the ship and pulled it to the landing berth. When the troops were aboard, the tug pulled the ship out to where it could safely navigate on its own power. How that little tug cold move that heavily loaded ship was beyond me.

As it had been with Korea, soon Japan began to recede into the background. As I watched it grow dimmer, I found myself reminiscing over R.&.R., my stay at the Rakuyo Hotel, and my walks to downtown Kyoto. I recalled the Japanese I met like Mr. Keru, who invited me to sit awhile while we drank a cold beer, who showed genuine concern over the way Koreans were treated by the Japanese military during the occupation, and who went to great pains to make sure I understood how prostitution fit into Japanese culture. He expressed a strong desire to visit the U.S. I hope he made it. It wasn't long after I returned to the States that prostitution was outlawed in Japan, largely because of pressure from the American Military. I often wondered what happened to the many girls who earned their living selling sex. "By golly, if you aren't like American society on this issue, you had better darn well become so in a big hurry."

And, of course, the very fond memories of Setsuko, that kind and gentle and very cute young woman who recognized my loneliness, befriended me and kept me company in Kyoto for most of seven days. How my feelings for her began to change in a way which frightened me since I was committed and could not let myself go, and how she developed strong feelings for me though I'm sure that wasn't in her plans either. And the painful parting at the depot across from the Rakuyo Hotel. I would never see her again. Though she is an elderly woman now, I have a picture I took of her, a good picture, and because of that picture, she will remain ever young to me.

The journey across the ocean was uneventful. Of course, as was the case when I sailed to Korea, I was nauseated for the entire 14 days it took to sail from Korea to Seattle. Because of the nausea, I couldn't eat and lost about 20 pounds. I was fortunate to escape K.P. and all other duties, which gave me opportunity to spend time on the upper deck when the weather permitted. Inspections, however, even on ship, went on. Frequently all troops were herded onto the upper deck while the officers inspected the "living" quarters.

One night I remember vividly. It was about 3:00 a.m. when I awoke in a panic. It seemed that the full impact of the reality of my coming marriage hit me for the first time. I remember thinking, "This really can't be about to happen to me; I'm really not going to be married in a few days after arriving home. Why, we are practically strangers to each other." I was in a cold sweat. I walked up on deck and spent hours pacing back and forth. I couldn't understand my feeling and panic since this is what I had been hoping, planning and praying for the past 16 months. "Why in the world am I panicking like this?" By daybreak, those feelings had passed completely and once again I was at peace with our wedding plans. I still wonder, what was there in my sleep that triggered that so unexpected reaction on my part?

On the 14th day after setting sail from Inchon, I began to see the dim outline of the American and Canadian west coasts. It was a sight to behold with high mountains seeming to leap straight up out of the water. Because this was June, the mountains still had much snow on them. How in the world does one explain the feeling at seeing American soil once again after an absence of so many months? We sailed into the Strait of San Juan de Fuca and, as we did, schools of dolphins ahead of the ship leaped in and out of the water as if to provide us with a most interesting escort. This was a first for me. When the ship left San Francisco, I saw no dolphin.

The Marine Serpent took a right turn and we headed for Puget Sound. Upon reaching port just outside of Fort Lewis, it anchored. The time was about 4:00 p.m. All troops had dressed in Class A uniforms, except those men held back to clean up all of the living compartments that had been occupied by approximately 3000 troops. We were herded onto the upper deck If I had fainted, I cound not have fallen to the deck. That is how closely we were packed together. Though U.S. soil was only a few hundred feet away, I would not set foot on good old American tera firma for another 18 hours. I along with all the other men, would spend the night up on that deck, crowded so close together. And, once we were on the upper deck, we were not allowed to return to the compartments we had occupied. I can't recall if we had opportunity to use the restrooms on ship or not. Seems to me none were available to us. But they had to be.

As the evening sun began to set, I could see Mount Rainier off to the east and south. It was a long way off but still visible and painted red by the rays of the setting sun. Simply stated, it was beautiful.

The night on the deck was long and cold but huddled as close together as we were, I don't think anyone got too cold. We were home, so who cared about being a little cold?

The early morning edition of the Seattle Post Intelligencer, Tuesday, June 29, 1954, headlined in big bold letters, read, "Marine Serpent Arrives with 3,044 GIs."

As the morning of June 29th dawned, the streets I could see came alive with people going to work, shopping, etc. One of the first things that impressed me was the obesity of the people. I was not prepared for this since obesity was something I did not see either in Korea or Japan. It was something I would have to get used to. And this was 1954, not 2000 when we are told that 60 percent of the American people are overweight.

Finally at 10:00 a.m., we began debarking and we did so in haste. How well I recall walking down the gangplank and setting foot on American soil. It was a great feeling. I immediately boarded a waiting bus for the short trip to Fort Lewis. Processing began at once and would continue until 4:00 p.m.

At Inchon, we were told that loved ones and friends should not plan to meet us at Fort Lewis, and at Fort Lewis we were told that loved ones and friends should not plan to meet us at the camp from which we would be discharged. Bonnie planned to meet me at Camp Carson (now Fort Carson), Colorado. I called her with this information and it was then that she said she would meet me at Schuyler, Nebraska. The conversation was brief but it was so good to hear her voice. Now I really wanted to get to Schuyler in haste.

From 4:00 p.m. until 10:00 p.m., I just waited around for my plane which would leave for Camp Carson promptly at 10:00 p.m. That seemed like a long, long wait. While processing at Fort Lewis, we had been told that we would fly commercial with a meal on the plane and stewardesses in attendance. We were looking forward to visiting with the stewardesses. Once again the military didn't get it quite right. I boarded a rickety old plane that was part of a shuttle service that ferried men from Fort Lewis to camps in the West. At times the way the plane shook and rattled, I wondered if I was going to make it to Camp Carson.

We landed at an isolated landing strip close to Camp Carson in the very early hours of June 30th. No one was there to meet those of us on the plane so I stretched out on the concrete runway, laid my head on my duffel bag and slept for a couple of hours. I had now been up for 44 hours. It wasn't until 8:00 a.m. that buses from Camp Carson arrived at the airstrip to take us to the Camp. Again, processing began immediately. The 4th of July weekend was just a couple of days away and the personnel at Camp Carson wanted to get us processed and out of there so they could have the weekend free. Processing was non stop. After it was all over, Except for the couple of hours of sleep on the runway, I figured I had been awake for over 70 hours.

Processing continued without let up. Records and items of clothing issued in Inchon, were checked. There were speeches including one that reminded me that I had served only two years of a 10 year hitch in the Army. I had an additional 8 years to serve in the Stand by Reserves. That came as quite a surprise, a rather revolting one. That meant that in the event of a national emergency, I could again find myself in uniform. The closest I came to that was the Lebanon crisis that erupted a few years later. I was encouraged to activate my reserve status by attending weekly meetings. That advice I declined.

Processing went on through the night of July 1. Finally, at about 4:00 p.m. on the afternoon of the 2nd, it was finished. With so many hours without sleep, I was in a daze and felt like I was on a very cheap drunk. Nonetheless, I made it to Denver and to the train depot. I boarded the train early and tried to get comfortable. The first thing I discovered was that it was cold in the train car, and it would remain cold for the entire 11 hours it took to reach Schuyler, Nebraska. Good gosh, it was chilly outside and the air conditioner was on. In addition, my Reynaud's didn't help matters any. As tired as I was, it was too cold to sleep. The hours of sleeplessness would continue.

At approximately 6:30 a.m., the train stopped at the depot in Schuyler. I was the only one to step off. The train continued on to Omaha. In the early morning, I was left alone on the depot platform. The depot was locked so I could not enter. I looked around for Bonnie, who was supposed to have been at the depot when I arrived, but I could not see her anywhere. Her absence was a keen disappointment. To say I was nervous was an understatement. We had sustained our love for 16 months through letters alone. Would we feel the same once we came face-to-face? We wrote about the possibility that after so many months, we might seem like strangers to each other. So many questions, so much anxiety. I started pacing back and forth on the depot platform. And then Bonnie was coming around a corner of the depot. I had asked her to wear red, red being my favorite color on her. She looked dazzling in red especially as it contrasted with her black, shining hair. And she was indeed wearing red and the rays of the early morning sun were doing a dance on her head. As I started walking to meet her, my heart skipped a beat. To my weary and sleepless eyes, she looked beautiful. It had been so long. As we anticipated, we did feel a bit like strangers in each others presence. In a moment, however, she was in my arms and our kiss was long and passionate. Any strangeness quickly slipped from us like the elusive morning breeze playing among the trees surrounding the depot. After sixteen long months, I knew I was really home.

ABOUT THE AUTHOR

Richard H. Waltner

After finishing his time in the Army, the author enrolled in the University of South Dakota where he received both his bachelors and masters degrees. Following graduation be taught for eight years at a small church related college in South Dakota. He then accepted a position in sociology at Montana State University, Billings. Concommitant to his move to Montana he enrolled in the University of Utah where he received his Ph.D., also in sociology. Upon his return to the University at Billings, he focused his studies and research efforts on the newly emerging field of human sexuality developing and teaching a variety of courses. After 39 years Dr. Waltner retired from active college teaching. He and his wife Bonnie have two sons and live near Park City, Montana.